Pilgrim to Rome

H.J. RICHARDS

PILGRIM ᴛᴏ ROME

A PRACTICAL GUIDE

Drawings by
CLARE RICHARDS

McCRIMMONS
Great Wakering, Essex

First published in Great Britain in 1994 by
McCRIMMON PUBLISHING CO. LTD.
10-12 High Street, Great Wakering, Essex SS3 0EQ
Tel: (0702) 218956; Fax: (0702) 216082

ISBN 0 85597 532 6

Illustrations by Clare Richards
Cover design by Nick Snode
Edited by Sue Simpson

Cover photograph of the Colosseum supplied by Zefa.
Cover background taken from the map of Rome generously supplied by Ente
Provinciale per il Turismo di Roma.

Typeset in 10pt New Baskerville and 11pt Newtext Demi by McCrimmons
Printed on 80gsm white offset, and 240gsm Invercote G.
Reproduction of Halftones by Anagram Litho Ltd, Southend–on–sea
Printed by Black Bear Press Ltd, Cambridge

This book is for
Mark, Chad and Dock,
Shell, Wat and Duck,
Charley, Tolly and Bricky,
in whose blessed company
I first trod
these sacred stones.

CONTENTS

ACKNOWLEDGEMENTS

Biblical quotations, except where noted, have been taken from the *Revised Standard Version of the Bible*, copyrighted 1952, HarperCollins Publishers Ltd. Reproduced with permission.

We also thank the following copyright holders for permission to use their material:

AA Publishing: for the extract on p.106. Reproduced from *AA/Baedeker Guide to Rome*, with permission of The Automobile Association.

Bible texts on pp.58 & 124. Taken from the *New Jerusalem Bible*, published and copyright 1985 by Darton, Longman and Todd Ltd and Doubleday & Co Inc, and used by permission of the publishers.

Chapman, Geoffrey: for the passage from *A Christian's Prayer Book*, p.62 (Cassell plc)

Clark, Eleanor: for the passage on p.101 *Rome and A Villa*, 1974, published by Aidan Ellis.

Day Lewis, C.: text on pp.113–114 from An Italian Visit, 1953 (Jonathan Cape Ltd.)

De Rosa, Peter: the prayer on p93, from *A Bible Prayer Book for Today*, Fontana, 1976 (an imprint of HarperCollins). Reproduced with permission.

TS Eliot: Choruses from 'The Rock', *Rock VI*, on p.50 (Faber & Faber Ltd).

The Grail: *The Psalms: A New Translation* (HarperCollins Publishers Ltd). Reproduced with permission.

Hilton, D.: two passages on pp.127, & 147 from *Liturgy of Life*, published by the National Christian Education Council.

Lundy, Damian: *Sing of a Girl* (v.1 only) p.147, and *Laudato sii, o mi Signore*, p.150 (Kevin Mayhew Ltd).

Micklem, Caryl, ed: prayers from *Contemporary Prayers for Public Worship*, SCM Press 1967.

HV Morton: *A Traveller in Rome*, 1957 (Methuen & Co Ltd).

Oosterhuis, Huub: from *Ten Table Prayers*. (Gooi en Sticht bv, exclusive agent for the English–language countries: OCP Publications).

Staniforth, Maxwell: on p.54, *Early Christian Writings: the Apostolic Fathers*, (Penguin Classics, 1968).

Hymn Section

Most of the hymns are taken from *The Complete Celebration Hymnal with New Songs of Celebration*, published by McCrimmon Publishing Co Ltd.

We acknowledge with thanks the following copyright holders:
Cassell plc for *This joyful Eastertide*; Copycare Ltd, administrators for *God forgave my sin*, *Holy, holy, holy* (Lexicon Music), *Jesus is Lord* (Springtide/Word Music) *Rejoice in the Lord* (Sacred Songs) and *Seek ye first* (Maranatha! Music); T. Dudley-Smith for *Tell out, my soul*; Franciscan Communications for *Make me a channel of your peace*; GIA Publications for *Take our bread*; Kevin Mayhew Ltd for *Do not be afraid*, *He did no wrong*, *Holy Virgin, by God's decree*, *Lamb of God*, and *Walk in the light*; Moody Press for *Spirit of the living God*; New Dawn Music (with JB Foley, SJ) for *If God is for us*; Oxford University Press for *Now the green blade riseth* (from the *Oxford Book of Carols*); Srs of St Mary of Namur for *O living water*, and *Word made flesh*; Stainer & Bell Ltd for *I danced in the morning*, and *When I needed a neighbour*; Thankyou Music for *Bind us together*, *How lovely on the mountains*, *I will sing, I will sing*, *Let there be peace* and *O Lord, my God*; Vanguard Music for *God's Spirit*; World Library Publications for *Keep in mind*; and World Student Christian Federation for *Thine be the glory, risen, conquering Son*.

Every effort has been made to trace the owners of copyright material, and we hope that no copyright has been infringed. Pardon is sought and apology made if the contrary be the case, and a correction will be made in any reprint of this book.

PRAYER FOR PILGRIMS

Our Father in heaven
you are the aim and object of our lives,
and the goal of our pilgrimage,
for you have made us for yourself
and our hearts are restless until they rest in you.
Show us again the way
along which our pilgrimage must travel,
for your son Jesus is the way that leads to you.
It is by following him,
by identifying ourselves with him,
by suffering with him and rising with him,
that we know we are on the right path.
Help us never to stray from that path,
but to walk in the footsteps he has marked out for us,
as all the martyrs and saints have done before us.
Amen.

FOREWORD

After I have been to Jerusalem, I must also see Rome. (*Acts 19: 21*)

Having written a pilgrim guide to the Holy Land which many have found helpful, I am delighted that my publishers have taken heed of this piece of advice from St Paul, and invited me to write a companion volume on Rome. Those who have walked the streets of Jerusalem and the lanes of Galilee in the footsteps of Christ will do well (if they can afford it) to complete their pilgrimage in Rome, and walk in the footsteps also of those first Christians who brought the good news of Jesus to this centre of the Roman Empire, from where it spread throughout Europe, and from there to the rest of the world.

I have tried to write this guidebook in the same style as the first, neither underrating nor overrating how much average pilgrims can take. Too much detail can diminish their interest rather than arouse it. Too little can kill it all together. A balance is needed, and I hope readers will tell me where this is lacking, so that future readers can benefit from corrections. I have also been conscious that, while pilgrims need to appreciate the distinction between Caracalla and Caravaggio, they have other needs too: food and drink, transport and toilets, and above all gift shops. These are as much part of a Roman pilgrimage as a papal audience.

Like the guide to the Holy Land, this book includes a selection of hymns which pilgrims may wish to sing should the occasion call for it, or simply use for meditation; and also a section containing resource material for worship, out of which a eucharistic service can be devised. The biblical quotations scattered through the book are inevitably fewer than those appropriate for the Holy Land, where the events spoken of in the text actually took place. But I hope the few dozen I have suggested, and the occasional prayers inserted into the text, will help readers deepen their understanding of the sites they have come to visit, not merely as tourists, but as pilgrims.

My warm thanks are due to the staff and students of the English College in Rome for their generous hospitality and eagerness to correct my mistakes, and to my wife Clare for the drawings and vignettes which enliven the pages that follow. They demonstrate, more clearly than my text, what a treasured place Rome holds in our hearts.

Travelling is the ruin of all happiness: there's no looking at a building here after seeing Italy.

(*Fanny Burney*, writer, 1752-1840)

INTRODUCTION

You may never have heard of Rome. But you've all heard of Lazio – the team Gazza plays for. Rome is simply the capital city of Lazio.   *Sports commentator*

A LITTLE GEOGRAPHY

For most people, the word Rome means Mediterranean. It is, of course true that Italy is a Mediterranean country, but newcomers might need a word of caution. Rome lies on latitude 42° north, on a level with Istanbul and New York, and is not in the same league as Alexandria (31°) or Tel Aviv (32°) or Beirut (34°). This means that its winters, though milder than English ones, are still wintry, and can have long rainy spells (Rome has 22cm more rain than London). Its summers too, though hot to the point of stickiness, can have very cool evenings, where wraps and sweaters are not out of place.

This being said, Rome is blessed with an enviable climate. Even in winter there are long periods of brilliant sunshine, and even in high summer the delightful cool of the early morning and late evening provide a welcome relief from the midday heat, during which all sensible people take a siesta. Most visitors choose to come to Rome in spring or autumn, when it is neither too hot nor too cold. But of course it will be more crowded.

	Temperature		Rainfall
Christmas	40-55°F	(5-13°C)	75-90cm
Easter	45-66°F	(7-19°C)	60-80cm
Midsummer	67-87°F	(20-30°C)	5-40cm
Oct-Nov	49-55°F	(9-13°C)	120-125cm

When Rome was at the height of its imperial power, its population is calculated to have been over a million. Numbers began to decline during Rome's 'dark ages', sometimes drastically. Even in renaissance times the city had no more than 50,000 inhabitants. Numbers remained low for many centuries, and it was not until the kingdom of Italy was formed that Rome again attracted a large population. By 1870 its numbers had climbed back to 200,000, and by 1920 to half a million. Recent immigration has raised this figure to close on three million.

A LITTLE HISTORY

Rome has played such a central role in the political, cultural and religious history of Europe that its story cannot be told simply without crass over-simplification. Rather than attempt such a task, I here offer a simple list of headings, dates and cross-references, in the hope that bewildered pilgrims will find it helpful.

Date	Rome	Elsewhere	The Arts
BC753	Foundation of Rome	Assyrian Empire Isaiah	Homer
	1. MONARCHY Etruscan kings	Exile of Israel	
586		Babylonian Empire Exile of Jews	
550	Servian Walls	Persian Empire	Pythagoras
510	**2. REPUBLIC** Latin League	Buddha	Aeschylus Euripides Sophocles
396	Expansion into Etruria		
390	Gauls invade		Plato
330		Alexander the Great	Aristotle Greek Empire
250	Expansion into Italy Punic War I		Euclid
	Expansion into Sicily	Great Wall of China	
219	Punic War II		
	Expansion into Spain		
202	Hannibal defeated		
168	Expansion into Greece	Maccabees	
149	Punic War III Carthage destroyed Expansion into N. Africa		
133	Rome controls Mediterranean		
66	Expansion into Asia Minor & Syria		
60	Pompey, Crassus, Caesar		
58	Expansion into Gaul Forays into Britain		Cicero
45	Caesar Dictator		
43	Mark Antony, Lepidus, Octavian		
31	Battle of Actium Expansion into Egypt	Herod	
30	Octavian=Emperor Augustus		Virgil Ovid Livy Horace Pantheon porch
	3. EMPIRE		
6			Birth of Jesus
AD14	Tiberius		

Date	Rome	Elsewhere	The Arts
30		Death of Jesus	
37	Caligula		Seneca
41	Claudius		
43	Expansion into Britain		
49		Journeys of Paul	
54	Nero	Persecution of Christians	
61	Paul in Rome		
64	Great Fire of Rome Death of Peter		
67	Death of Paul		
69	Vespasian	Destruction of Jerusalem Masada	
79	Titus Vesuvius		Tacitus Juvenal Martial
81	Domitian	Persecution of Christians	Plutarch
96	Nerva		
98	Trajan		Pliny
116	Expansion into Armenia & Mesopotamia		
117	Hadrian	Hadrian's Wall Jerusalem = Aelia Capitolina	Pantheon Castel S. Angelo
132		Last Jewish Revolt	Hadrian's Villa
161	Marcus Aurelius		
193	Septimius Severus		Arch of Severus
212	Caracalla		Caracalla Baths
220	Arab invasions		
270	Aurelian Walls		
284	Diocletian	Persecution of Christians	
306	Constantine with Maxentius		
312	Constantine alone		
313	Edict of Milan Freedom of worship for Christians		Christian basilicas
325		Council of Nicaea	
330	Move from Rome to Byzantium		
349		Ambrose	
380	Christianity=state religion		
410	Invasion of Goths	Augustine	
440	Pope Leo the Great = new Emperor?	Patrick	

Date	Rome	Elsewhere	The Arts
455	Vandals sack Rome	Anglo-Saxons invade Britain	
476	Collapse of Western Empire		

4. THE 'DARK AGES'

Date	Rome	Elsewhere	The Arts
480	Ravenna capital of Italy		
524		Benedict	Boethius
568	Invasion of Lombards	Columba	
590	Pope Gregory the Great assumes control of Rome	Evangelisation of pagan England	
600		Muhammad Cuthbert	
720			Bede
730		Arabs invade Spain & France	
754		Franks invade Italy	
773		Charlemagne unites Lombards & Franks	Alcuin
800	Pope Leo III crowns Charlemagne		

5. 'HOLY ROMAN EMPIRE'

Date	Rome	Elsewhere	The Arts
846	Saracens sack Rome		
871		Alfred the Great	
879	Rome & Constantinople excommunicate each other		
1000	Normans invade Italy	Vikings invade America	
1054	East-West schism		
1066		Normans invade England	
1073	Pope Gregory VII Hildebrand Struggle with emperors for supremacy		Anselm
1095		First Crusade	
1115			Abelard
1152	Emperor Frederick I Barbarossa	Thomas à Becket	
1154	English pope Adrian IV		
1184	Creation of 'Holy' Inquisition	Richard Lionheart	Cosmati Family
1200		Genghis Khan Fourth Crusade Francis of Assisi Dominic	
1215		Magna Carta	
1265	French control of S. Italy		Thomas Aquinas

16

Date	Rome	Elsewhere	The Arts
	6. EARLY RENAISSANCE		
1300	Popes & emperors in power struggle	Marco Polo	Cimabue Giotto Dante Boccaccio Petrarch
1309	Popes emigrate to Avignon		Botticelli
1362	Hospice for English pilgrims		Titian Perugino
		Catherine of Siena	Cavallini
1377	Popes return to Vatican		Chaucer
1378	Popes and anti-popes	Wyclif	
1429		Joan of Arc	Van Eyck
1453		Sack of Constantinople	Angelico
	7. HIGH RENAISSANCE		
1492	Pope Alexander VI Borgia	Columbus in America	Caxton da Vinci Bramante
1503	Pope Julius II Sistine Chapel		Michelangelo
	Raphael Rooms	Martin Luther	Raphael Savanarola
1521		Machiavelli Protestant Reformation	Erasmus
1527	Sack of Rome by German imperial troops		
	Sistine 'Last Judgement'	Henry VIII	
1538	Ignatius Loyola in Rome	Fisher and More	
1545	Council of Trent		Copernicus
	Building of St Peter's		
1560		Elizabeth I	Tallis
		39 Articles	Palestrina
1571		Turks repelled at Lepanto	
1579	Venerable English College	Francis Drake	
1588		Spanish Armada	
	8. BAROQUE AGE		
1600			Shakespeare Byrd Donne Cervantes
1605		Guy Fawkes	Caravaggio Reni Monteverdi Maderna

17

Date	Rome	Elsewhere	The Arts
1620		Pilgrim Fathers in America	Bernini Borromini
1633	Galileo in Rome		Milton
1660	St Peter's Square	Charles II	Newton
1666		Great Fire of London	Bunyan Handel Fontana Scarlatti
1688		William of Orange	Vivaldi
1720			Wren
1730		John Wesley	Alexander Pope
1735	Spanish Steps		Bach Swift Voltaire Canova
1776		American Declaration of Independence	Haydn
1789		George Washington French Revolution	Mozart
1796	Napoleon takes Rome Papal States confiscated		Byron Kant

9. NINETEENTH CENTURY

Date	Rome	Elsewhere	The Arts
1805	End of Holy Roman Empire Decline of papal power	Trafalgar	Wordsworth Goethe Goya
1814	Congress of Vienna Papal States restored		Beethoven
1815	Keats & Shelley in Rome	Waterloo	Schubert
1829		Catholic Emancipation	Chopin
			Brontë Sisters
1831	'Risorgimento' movement		Pugin
1837		Queen Victoria	
1846	Pope Pius IX J.H. Newman in Rome		Verdi Rossini
1848		Marx's Communist Manifesto	
1854		Crimean War Lourdes	Dickens Wagner
1859			Darwin
1861	Garibaldi & Cavour Italy united Victor Emmanuel II king	American Civil War	V. Hugo
1869	Vatican Council	Suez Canal built	Brahms
1870	Papal infallibility Rome capital of Italy		Dostoevski Wilde

Date	Rome	Elsewhere	The Arts
1870	End of Papal States		Puccini
	Pope 'prisoner of Vatican'		Tennyson
1878	Pope Leo XIII		Browning
1899		Boer War	Freud
			Renoir
			Cézanne
			Elgar

10. TWENTIETH CENTURY

Date	Rome	Elsewhere	The Arts
1900	Victor Emmanuel III king	Edward VII	Zola
			Tolstoy
			Marconi
1903	Pope Pius X		H.G.Wells
			Kipling
1914	Pope Benedict XV	World War I	G.M.Hopkins
1921		Irish Free State	Matisse
1922	Pope Pius XI		Shaw
	Mussolini Dictator		Holst
1929	Lateran Treaty		Picasso
	Creation of Vatican City		T.S.Eliot
1933		Hitler	
1935		Italy invades Abyssinia	Cocteau
1936		Edward VIII	D.H.Lawrence
		Rome-Berlin Axis	
		Spanish Civil War	Hemingway
1939	Pope Pius XII	World War II	Coward
1943		Allies invade Italy	Waugh
			Sartre
1944	Rome liberated		Camus
1945	Mussolini assassinated		
1946	Victor Emmanuel III abdicates		Britten
1948	Italian Republic	Creation of State of Israel	Auden
1956		Suez crisis	Pasternak
1957	EEC and Treaty of Rome		Hitchcock
1958	Pope John XXIII		Greene
1961		Berlin Wall	
1962	Council of Vatican II		
1963	Pope Paul VI	Kennedy assassinated	
1978	Popes John Paul I & II		
1981	Assassination attempt on pope		
1982		Falklands War	
1989		Collapse of Soviet Union	
		Gulf War	
1991		Civil War in Yugoslavia	
1993		Israel acknowledges Palestine	

DOCUMENTS

Travellers to Italy need either an updated passport or a temporary visitor's pass. Visas for short-term visitors from the UK, USA or Canada are no longer required, nor are inoculations. Travel agents will be able to advise about insurance. A package deal comprising accident, delay, money, medical, curtailment, liability, cancellation and baggage, would seem to be the best.

HEALTH

Those who are on a prescribed régime will presumably take their own drugs with them: chemists in Rome are expensive. The change of weather and diet gives some people 'tummy'; this can generally be overcome with Imodium or Arrêt or something similar. Iced drinks and coffee should be avoided during this distressing time, but tea and lemon can be helpful.

Those liable to sunburn should take their own lotion. Those exhausted by the heat may find relief with half a teaspoon of salt in water. Aspirins, kwells and footpowder hardly need mentioning, but people may need to be told of the benefits of wax earplugs if they have to share a room.

ACCESS FROM THE AIRPORT

Leonardo da Vinci airport is near the coast at Fiumicino, 35km from Rome. There is a train every 20 minutes for the 20 minute journey to the Ostiense station (cost about £3), from which the Metro line B continues the journey into the town centre. Taxis from the airport to the city centre take 30-40 minutes, and will cost about £30.

Ciampino airport, mainly used by charter flights, is only 15km from Rome. ACOTRAL buses run every half hour to the southern terminal of Metro A, on which the journey can be continued into town. There are ticket machines for both legs of the journey, which together cost about £1. A taxi will cost about £18.

TRANSPORT

The area of Rome that most visitors are interested in is not large – only about 3km square, and the heart of it is only 1km across. Most sightseeing is therefore most conveniently done on foot, not only because of the dense traffic, but because the back lanes behind the main thoroughfares are often the most picturesque.

For greater distances, Rome's ATAC bus service (6.00-24.00) is both efficient and cheap. Tickets are not available on board, but must be purchased beforehand at a tobacconist or news kiosk, at about 1000 lire (50p) each. They are valid for as many journeys as can be fitted into 90 minutes, and should be time-punched on the first and last buses boarded. Entrance is from the rear, and exit from the middle. There are also a few tramlines which operate on the same principle. Tram no. 30 is ideal for an extensive and leisurely tour of the city. Take a map.

Recently two underground lines (5.30-23.30) have been burrowed through the city, one (line A) running from near Ciampino airport to the Vatican, and the other (line B) from the far north – east of the city to the EUR. They are known as the *Metropolitana*. They cross at the main rail station of Termini, where you may change lines. Tickets for any journey, long or short, are 1000 lire (50p) each, and are obtained at tobacconists, kiosks, or ticket machines at the station. 'BIG' tickets, valid for the whole day on buses as well, are available at ATAC and Metro ticket booths at 3,000 lire (£1.50).

Plan of the Rome Metro

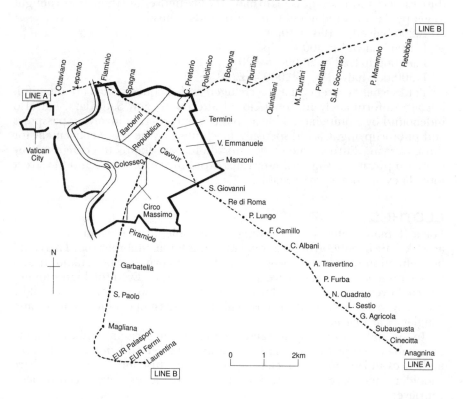

For taxi journeys, it is safest to use the metered yellow cabs only (private cabs are exorbitant and uninsured). There are many ranks for these in the city, but they can be called by phone for a small supplement. It is best to establish the fare before embarking, but expect to pay 6,000 lire (£3) as a starting price, and a further £1 for the shortest journey. Luggage and night travel, of course, add to the cost.

More colourful journeys by *carozza* (horse-drawn carriage) should be negotiated with the driver. An hour's drive can cost 100,000 lire (£50).

MONEY

The Italian economy overtook the British in 1987, and has stayed ahead ever since. This means that whereas Italy used to be one of the cheapest places for Britons to take a holiday, it is now one of the dearest. Be prepared for high prices: a small espresso coffee can cost 50p or more, and a small bottle of beer up to £2.

For some time the exchange rate has fluctuated around 2,000 lire for the pound (£) – if it is higher you gain, if lower you lose. If it remains at this level, the easiest way to assess prices is to halve the lire figure, and then drop a nought to get pence, or three noughts to get pounds. Thus:

L.200 halved = 100 = 10p
L.1,000 halved = 500 = 50p
L.40,000 halved = 20,000 = £20
L.500,000 halved = 250,000 = £250.

Banks where currency may be changed and cheques cashed are plentiful, but are unfortunately not only closed afternoons and Saturdays, but also hidebound by a quite incredible amount of bureaucracy involving passports and photocopying. Cash dispensing machines may be more convenient for those carrying Eurocheque cards. Most hotels are happy to change money more simply, if at a slightly lower rate. Avoid the small *cambio* and the street tout. They are not always reliable.

CLOTHES

For a Roman winter warm clothing is advisable, as well as an overcoat or anorak. The likelihood of occasional rain calls for an umbrella too. This could be useful in summer as well, when short thunderstorms are not unknown, and plastic raincoats are useless because of the humidity. Even the high summer has cool evenings (and cool churches) for which a sweater or a wrap will be useful, even when the daytime has made the lightest of clothing, sunhats and sunglasses *de rigueur*.

In the high season of spring and autumn, the most casual clothes are quite acceptable, except in high-class restaurants (jacket and tie), and at papal audiences and in churches (including the Vatican Museum), where shorts, bare shoulders and bare arms are forbidden. Bare heads have recently been reprieved.

Sensible shoes are advisable even for those who visit by taxi, since basilicas, museums and catacombs can involve a good deal of walking.

Mention should be made, under this heading of clothes, of the current Roman epidemic of bagsnatching and pickpocketing, especially by the children of impoverished gypsies. Shoulder bags are safer than handbags, the sturdier the better (even camera straps have been slashed), and the more zipped the more secure. It is sensible to carry with you only the money, documents and cheques you actually need, and even these are safer in a bodybelt or bumbag than in a wallet. To leave a shoulder bag unattended, even to take a snap, is to ask for trouble.

CAFÉS

No one can continue sightseeing for hours on end without a break. Rome offers a thousand breaks in its inviting cafés, which all offer not only coffee but a variety of drinks and eats. Newcomers need to be informed that you decide what you want and pay for it at the till first, before presenting the chit at the counter for your purchase, which most people consume standing. To sit at a table and ask for waiter service will increase the bill fourfold. Avoid cafés in the most frequented tourist spots, which are very expensive.

Cafés are usually the most convenient place from which to make local phone calls. Some of the phones work on a token coin (*gettone*), obtainable from the cashier for 200 lire (10p), though these are slowly being phased out in favour of coins or phone-cards.

CHURCHES

Rome's main basilicas (St Peter, St Paul, St John Lateran, St Mary Major) are open all day. Other churches are liable to be closed from 12.00-15.00, although they then remain open till dusk. Because of the restoration work which has been underway since 1980, and from which many churches have already benefited, some churches may be shrouded in sheets and scaffolding, or even temporarily closed. It is worth checking before visiting. Many churches now have their masterpieces illuminated by a timed slot-machine, for which it is useful to have spare coins (100 and 200 lire) available. And note the embargo on dress mentioned above.

Permission to celebrate Mass in these churches should be obtained beforehand, and an offering left. Sunday services in English (but check the times) are available at:

S. Silvestro in Capite (see p.128).
English College (see p.63).
S. Clemente (Irish Dominicans, see p.52).
S. Isidoro (Irish Franciscans), Via Ludovisi.
St Patrick (Irish Augustinians), Via Buoncompagni.
S. Susanna (American Paulists), Via XX Settembre.

Non-Catholic services are held at:
All Saints (Church of England) Via del Babuino 153.
Baptist Church, Via Urbana 154.
St Paul's (American Episcopal), near the top of Via Nazionale.
American Methodist Church, Via Firenze 38.
Jewish Synagogue, Lungotevere near the Island.
Greek Orthodox Church, Via Sardegna 153.

MUSEUMS

There are 70 museums in Rome. The most popular ones are listed below under their proper name, with the opening times currently advertised. These times are however subject to change, and it would be wise to check before a proposed visit. Many are closed on one day a week, usually Monday. Admission charges tend to be fairly steep, between £3 and £5 a time. However the famous Vatican Museum has free admission for all comers on the last Sunday of each month; and the museums owned by the State (such as the Forum and Castel S. Angelo, etc) give free entrance at all times to the under 18's and the over 60's. Documentary evidence (eg passport) is needed. These State museums are all noted in their proper place below.

PAPAL AUDIENCE

All visitors to Rome are welcome to an 'audience' with the pope, if he is in residence, either in the city or at Castel Gandolfo. In the city he holds a public audience every Wednesday morning, either in St Peter's Square if the weather is appropriate, or in the new Audience Hall to the left, designed by Nervi in 1971, with its capacity for 7,000. For groups, arrangements are usually made by the travel agent. Individual pilgrims need to apply in advance, either by post (Prefettura Papale, Vatican City, Rome), or personally at the office of the same name at the end of the right colonnade nearest the basilica, open 9.00-13.00 (Wednesdays only until the audience begins). For English pilgrims, the English College (see p.63) can make the arrangements. An offering should be made for administration. Dress should be modest: those in shorts, or in sleeveless tops or short skirts, are turned away. The pope will usually greet the various groups by name, address them in their own language, and perhaps finish with a popemobile cruise round the piazza.

For more personal or private audiences, dress requirements are stricter still. Clothes should be formal and dark. Ladies should wear a mantilla or veil, not a hat. Arrangements for these special audiences should be made well in advance.

Those who are unable to attend these official audiences may wish to know that the pope appears at his window overlooking the piazza every Sunday at midday, to make a short speech and pray for God's blessing on those who have come. He may occasionally appear at midday on weekdays too, to pray the *Angelus* with those who have gathered.

FURTHER READING

Of making many guidebooks there is no end. (*Ecclesiastes 12: 12*)

Guidebooks to Rome have been produced ever since tourists have gone there in sufficient numbers to make such publications commercially viable. If the present project at Fiumicino goes ahead, to enable Rome's Leonardo da Vinci airport to handle 25 million passengers a year by 2000AD, then guidebooks will proliferate even more than they have done in the past. Here all I can do is to draw attention to those which I have found most helpful in preparing this book.

Karl Baedecker began producing meticulously accurate guidebooks to all parts of the world over a hundred years ago. His company continues to thrive, and its 1991 *Rome* (Jarrold and AA), though no longer as pedantically detailed as in the past, is a joy to handle. So too is the rival *Fodor's Rome* (1992), which is embellished by a number of fine supporting essays. Unfortunately it has opted to index its plans alphabetically rather than numerically, making them most tiresome to read, and its general index, half in Italian and half in English, is a hindrance rather than a help.

Three classic guides demand mention, all rich in history and anecdotes which bring dead stones to life: H.V. Morton's *A Traveller in Rome* (Methuen 1957), G. Masson's *Companion Guide to Rome* (Fontana 1972), and E.Clark's *Rome and a Villa* (Ellis 1974) – the latter marred by a nostalgia rather too frequently condemnatory of what has spoilt the author's cosy vision of the past.

Those whose interest in Christian Rome is deeper than this book can satisfy, may be helped by S.Luff's closely researched *The Christian's Guide to Rome* (Burns Oates 1990). And aficionados of ancient pre-Christian Rome will warm to the delightful visual aid provided by the folding transparencies in *Rome Past and Present*, (Vision, SRL 1962).

SUGGESTED ITINERARIES

The bewildered tourist who is flung into this whirlpool of history and association for two or three days and is expected to assimilate in that time the events of several thousands of years, how deeply he is to be pitied.

H.V. Morton, *A Traveller in Rome*, p.76

In the days of the 'Grand Tour', Karl Baedecker had no qualms about advising his readers that Rome could not possibly be appreciated in less than three or four weeks. His suggested itinerary is accordingly written on the assumption that drivers may be 'instructed to wait patiently until the clients are ready to rejoin the conveyance'.

Today's pilgrims are no longer blessed with such leisure or luxury, and must get Rome 'fitted into' a few days, perhaps a week for the fortunate, occasionally even ten days for *de luxe* travellers. Here, then, are some suggestions about how these days might be most profitably spent.

10 days

Day 1: THE TOMBS OF THE APOSTLES

After I have been to Jerusalem I must also see Rome. (*St Paul, Acts 19: 21*)

Up to Pincio (p.119) or the Janiculum (p.78) for a panorama of the city. On to St Peter's for a short visit, including the crypt (p.109), then on to St Paul's (p.107).

Afternoon free to return and ascend the dome of St Peter's.

Day 2: CLASSICAL ROME

The grandeur that was Rome. (*E.A. Poe*)

Capitol Hill (p.42) with St Mary Aracoeli to the left (p.87), and the Tarpeian Rock to the right (p.44). Down to the Mamertine Prison (p.86) and the Forum entrance.
Walk through the Forum (p.66) to the Arch of Titus, and exit to the Colosseum (p.55). Coach back to the hotel via the Pantheon (p.105) and Piazza Navona (p.100).

Afternoon free for Capitol Museum (p.43) (closed Mondays), or Palatine Hill (p.102), or Castel S. Angelo (p.44) (closed Mondays am), or Augustus Mausoleum and Ara Pacis (p.97) (closed Mondays), or National Museum (p.38) (closed Mondays).

Day 3: ROME AND THE EARLY CHRISTIANS

The whole army of martyrs praise Thee. (The *Te Deum*)

Mass at the Catacombs (p.46). Back into town for St Mary Major (p.90), St John Lateran (p.81) and the Scala Santa (p.83).

In the afternoon, some of the following could be visited:
On the Coelian Hill, St Clement (p.52), St Stephen (p.126), Quattro Coronati (p.121).
On the Aventine, St Mary Cosmedin (p.89), St Sabina (p.123).
Across the river, St Cecilia (p.50), St Mary Trastevere (p.95).
Back in town, Sts Cosmas and Damian (p.59).

Day 4: ROME AND THE ENGLISH

Some corner of a foreign field that is forever England. (*R.Brooke*)

Mass at St Gregory (p.76).
Venerable English College (p.63) and on to Farnese Palace (p.65), Spada Palace and Campo dei Fiori (p.40).
Walk through town to St Sylvester (English Catholics) (p.128), Piazza di Spagna (Keats) (p.118), All Saints Via Babuino (Anglicans) (p.23), and Flaminian Gate (Wiseman) (p.94).
The tour finishes at the Protestant Cemetery (Keats and Shelley) (p.39).

Day 5: (continued)
A day in the Alban Hills to visit the English College Villa at Palazzola (lunch can be arranged), Monte Cavo and Frascati (Stuart memorials), and the papal villa at Castel Gandolfo (p.142 ff).

Day 6: ROME AND THE ARTISTS

Art is a lie that makes us realise the truth. (*Picasso*)

Vatican Museum, Picture Gallery, and Sistine Chapel (p.133).

Afternoon free to visit the tomb of Fra Angelico in St Mary Minerva (p.92) and of Raphael in the Pantheon (p.105). Nearby there are Caravaggios in St Louis (p.85) and St Augustine (p.34). Also near is Bernini's fountain and Borromini's church of St Agnes in Piazza Navona (p.100), and the churches of St Ignatius (p.77) and the Gesù (p.73). Michelangelo's Moses (p.116), and Bernini's St Teresa (p.96) are further up town.

Day 7 & 8: ASSISI

Laudato sii, o mi Signore. (*St Francis*)

Coach via Orvieto cathedral to Assisi (p.146). Overnight.
Mass next day at one of the shrines, and a leisurely visit to the others. Return to Rome.
   An alternative day excursion could be made to Tivoli (p.145) or to Ostia (p.143), where there is swimming.

Day 9: FREE DAY

I never was good at sightseeing, yet it must be done. (*W.Wordsworth, 1837*)

A day should be left free for individuals to re-visit any of the above, to catch up on what they have missed, or to complete their shopping. They could all rendezvous at the Trevi Fountain (p.131) with their coins.
   Note that the papal audience (p.24), if there is to be one, must be fitted in. It is usually held on Wednesdays at 11.00.

Day 10: Last visits and purchases, and so on to the airport.

7 days

As above, combining days 4 and 5 into one, and days 7 and 8 into one, and omitting day 9.

5 days

Day 1: Combine days 1 and 2.
Day 2: As day 3 above.
Day 3: As day 4 above.
Day 4: As days 7 and 8 above.
Day 5: As day 9 above.

3 days

Day 1:A coach tour (including a panoramic view) to the Vatican Museum and Sistine Chapel (p.133), and then on to the four major basilicas (St Peter p.109, St Paul p.107, St Mary Major p.90, and St John Lateran p.81).

Day 2: The Catacombs (p.46), the Colosseum (p.55) and the Forum (p.66). An afternoon coach tour could include the English College (p.63), Piazza Navona (p.100), the Pantheon (p.105), and Piazza di Spagna (p.118).

Day 3:If time allows, the Assisi visit (p.146) should not be omitted.

1 day

For the visitor with only a day to savour Rome, Baedecker suggests a gentle stroll starting from the Colosseum (p.55), through the Forum (p.66) to the Monument and Piazza Venezia (p.98). From there the Corso (p.59), and the Via delle Muratte about 400m along on the right, lead to the Trevi Fountain (p.131). Returning to the Corso and crossing it, it is a short walk to the Pantheon (p.105), and from there to the Piazza Navona (p.100). The Corso Vittorio Emmanuele (p.59) leads to the Tiber, which can be crossed by the Ponte S. Angelo to the Castel S. Angelo (p.44). Turning left, there is an imposing view up the Via della Conciliazione which leads to St Peter's (p.109) and the Vatican (p.133).

This walking tour could profitably end with a stroll through Trastevere (p.130) and a meal in one of its many restaurants.

ESSENTIAL WORDS

above *sopra* (SOP-ra)
bad *cattivo* (ka-TEE-vo)
because *perche* (pair-KAY)
below *sotto* (SOT-toh)
closed *chiuso* (ki-OO-so)
cold *freddo* (FRED-oh)
don't understand *non capisco* (non cap-PEE-sko)
do you speak English? *parla inglese?* (par-la ing-LAY-seh?)
entrance *ingresso* (in-GRESS-oh)
excuse me *permesso* (pair-MESS-oh)
exit *uscita* (oo-SHEE-ta)
go away *via* (VEE-ah)
good *buono* (BWO-no)
here *qui* (kwee)
hot *caldo* (KAL-doh)
hotel *albergo* (al-BEAR-go)
how much? *quanto?* (KWAN-toh?)
left *sinistra* (si-NEES-tra)
less *meno* (MEN-oh)
little *poco* (POK-oh)
more *più* (pee-OOH)
much *molto* (MOLL-toh)
no *no*
open *aperto* (a-PAIR-toh)
please *per favore* (pair fav-ORR-eh)
postcard *cartolina* (cart-o-LEE-na)
right *destra* (DESS-tra)
sorry *scusi* (SKOO-see)
stamp *francobollo* (franko-BOLL-oh)
stop (enough!) *basta* (BASS-ta)
telephone *telefono* (tel-EFF-o-noh)
thank you *grazie* (GRA-tsee-eh)
there *la*
ticket *biglietto* (bill-YET-toh)
today *oggi* (ODGE-ee)
toilet *gabinetto* (gab-in-ETT-oh)
tomorrow *domani* (doh-MAH-nee)
too much *troppo* (TROP-oh)
water *acqua* (AH-kwa)
what? *che?* (kay?)
when? *quando?* (KWAN-doh)
where? *dovè?* (DOH-vay?)
who? *chi?* (kee?)
why? *perchè?* (pair-KAY?)
wine *vino* (VEE-no)
yes *si* (see)

ROME A TO Z

AGNES, St

see p.49 (Catacomb of) and p.100.

ALBANO, Lake

see p.142.

ALEXIS (Alessio)

see p.124.

ANDREW, churches of St. (S. Andrea)

Built on low-lying ground (*della valle*), the church of the apostle St Andrew on the Corso Vittorio Emmanuele (map F2) will probably stay immortal as the scene of the opening act in Puccini's *Tosca*. The baroque artists Maderna and Fontana co-operated to build it in the 17th century, and crowned it with a dome only a little smaller than St Peter's. This was decorated inside by Domenichino, and the walls and chapels still contain some extraordinarily fine paintings and statues, including those of the Renaissance Piccolomini popes Pius II and III. A long overdue municipal spring-clean of the exterior (1992) has restored this great church to its former glory, to the delight no doubt of the Theatine Fathers that run it.

There are two other churches of St Andrew in Rome. One was originally designed as the chapel for the adjoining Jesuit seminary, and then until 1946 served as the royal chapel for the Quirinal Palace opposite. **S. Andrea al Quirinale** (map E3) is the work of Bernini (1658): he considered it his finest, and his answer to his rival Borromini's masterpiece built 20 years earlier (see p.51). Small as it is, it has a monumental quality, the eight oval side chapels setting off to perfection the larger and lavish oval of the whole.

S. Andrea delle Fratte, just off the Via Tritone (map E3), also illustrates the rivalry between Borromini who built the belltower, and Bernini whose angels designed for the Ponte S. Angelo finished up decorating this church. The Gothic enthusiast Pugin, when told that Alphonse Ratisbonne was converted from Judaism to Christianity when our Lady appeared to him in this church, refused to believe that the Mother of God would visit such a baroque monstrosity.

John 1: 40-42: One of the two who heard John (Baptist) speak was Andrew, Simon Peter's brother. He first found his brother Simon, and said to him, 'We have found the Messiah' (which means Christ). He brought him to Jesus.

ANGLICAN CENTRE

see p.62.

ANSELM, College of St.

see p.125.

APOSTLES, Church of the Twelve. (Dodici Apostoli)

map F3

Rather overshadowed by the three Roman *palazzi* that hem it in, the church of the Holy Apostles was founded in the 6th century, but has been rebuilt and restored several times since. The 15th century porch is impressive, as are the sculptures by Mino da Fiesole (15th century) and Canova (18th century) inside. On a column in the nave is an urn that contains the heart of Clementina Sobieski, daughter of the Polish Sobieski who turned back the Turks at the gates of Vienna in 1683. Clementina married the Stuart prince James here in Rome (he gave her the Crown Jewels of England as an engagement present) and was the mother of bonnie Prince Charlie.

Luke 6: 12-16: Jesus went out to the mountain to pray; and all night he continued in prayer to God. And when it was day, he called his disciples, and chose from them twelve, whom he named apostles; Simon, whom he named Peter, and Andrew his brother, and James and John, and Philip, and Bartholomew, and Matthew, and Thomas, and James the son of Alphaeus, and Simon who was called the Zealot, and Judas the son of James, and Judas Iscariot, who became a traitor.

Roman Canon: In the unity of holy fellowship we reverence the memory... of thy blessed apostles and martyrs Peter and Paul, Andrew, James, John, Thomas, James, Philip, Bartholomew, Matthew, Simon and Thaddaeus...

APPIAN WAY (Via Appia)

map I4-L5 (See plan on p.47)

This 'Queen of the Roads' running southwest from Rome to Naples was built in 312BC by Appius Claudius, and so received his name.

The word *Antica* has been added to distinguish it from the *Via Appia Nuova* now running parallel some distance from it, and better geared to receive modern traffic arriving in Rome from this quarter.

Not that motorised traffic is absent from the old Appian Way. This once pleasant walk out into the Campagna, often no wider than a country lane without pavements, is nowadays more comfortably done on the 118 bus which plies regularly from the Lateran and Colosseum. Once outside the walls, the road shortly comes to the **Domine Quo Vadis** church (see p.61), and after only 2km stops at the **Catacombs of S. Callisto** (see p.48), and after another 600m at the **Catacombs of St Sebastian** (see p.48).

Just beyond St Sebastian, a large gateway on the left marks the entrance to the **Circus of Maxentius** (who also built the noble Basilica of Maxentius in the Forum, see p.70) in 309AD. It seated 18,000 spectators, and is still well enough preserved to give a good idea of what Roman chariot-racing was like. The obelisk now in the Piazza Navona once decorated the *spina* or central dividing wall.

Only 400m further on, also on the left, is the circular **Tomb of Cecilia Metella**, with pieces of sculptured marble still decorating the stone building. Cecilia was the daughter-in-law of Crassus, who with Caesar and Pompey formed the triumvirate of 60BC. The tomb, later turned into a fortress to exact tolls from travellers, marks the end of the bus line.

From here on the Via Appia, straight as an arrow in Roman fashion, makes its way through the Campagna, lined with cypresses, pines and lonely tombs, many of them still in a good state of preservation. A little distance away stand the noble arches of abandoned aqueducts. The road is occasionally paved with large blocks of basalt, the overflow of an eruption of what is now **Lake Albano** (see p.142). The marks of chariot wheels can still be seen in the molten rock, and may evoke memories of St Paul, who travelled this way to his imprisonment in Rome in AD61.

Between the Catacombs and Metella, there are a number of delightful country *trattorie* to refresh the weary pilgrim.

Acts 28: 13-15: On the second day we came to Puteoli (Pozzuoli), where we found brethren, and were invited to stay with them for seven days. And so we came to Rome. And the brethren there, when they heard of us, came as far as the Forum of Appius and Three Taverns to meet us. On seeing them Paul thanked God and took courage.

ARA PACIS
see p.97.

ARCH OF CONSTANTINE

Map FG3. Metro A, Colosseo.

Rome has a number of triumphal arches from the time of the emperors. They served no practical purpose, since they were only erected to march the troops through as they returned from war. Nonetheless they were thought a worthwhile tribute from the Roman Senate to the conquering hero. The arch of Constantine marks his victory over his rival for the throne, Maxentius (see pp.33 and 70) in 315AD. The date marks the end of hundreds of years of the persecution of Christians.

The arch is the largest and best preserved in Rome, with many magnificent decorative reliefs. Sadly, most of these have been 'borrowed' from the monuments of past emperors, either for the sake of economy, or because great sculptors were no longer as plentiful as in the old days.

> *Constantine*: We have long considered that freedom of worship should not be denied. Rather, each man's thoughts and desire should be granted him, thus enabling him to have regard for spiritual things as he himself may choose. This is why we have given orders that everyone should be allowed to have his own beliefs and worship as he wishes.
>
> (*Edict of Milan* AD313)

ARCH OF SEPTIMIUS SEVERUS
see p.68.

ARCH OF TITUS
see p.70.

ARDEATINE CAVES
see p.61.

ASSISI
see p.146.

AUGUSTINE, Church of St.

Piazza S. Agostino, near Piazza Navona. Map E2.

One of the many 15th century churches built from the mellow travertine stone once part of the Colosseum, St Augustine's underwent an interior rebuilding in the 18th century. It is famous for its Sansovino *Madonna del Parto* (1521) just inside the door, highly

popular (witness the foot worn smooth) with childless and expect-
ant mothers. The first chapel on the left has a moving *Madonna of
Loreto* by Caravaggio (1604), and further along by the third pillar
is another Sansovino group of the *Holy Family*. Above it, the pillar
bears a retouched fresco by Raphael. The high altar was designed
by Bernini, and to its left is the tomb of St Augustine's mother
Monica, whose remains were brought here from Ostia (see p.143).
The fine façade has recently (1992) been cleaned.

> *Giovanni Coricio, 1512*: When I told Michelangelo I had paid Raphael
> far too much for that fresco, he told me the knee alone was worth it.

> *Augustine, Confessions I, 1*:
> Thou hast created us for thyself, O God,
> And our heart is restless until it rests in thee.

> *Augustine, Commentary on John 8: 7*:
> If you really love, then you can do what you really want to do.

AUGUSTUS, MAUSOLEUM of.
see p.97.

AURELIAN WALL
see p.140.

BABINGTON'S
see p.118.

BAPTIST CHURCH
see p.23.

BARBERINI PALACE

> Via Quattro Fontane 13. Metro A, Barberini. Map
> E3. Open 9.00-14.00 (Sun to 13.00). Admission
> charge, except for under 18's and over 60's.

Bernini and Borromini co-operated with Maderna to produce this
sumptuous 17th century palace for the Barberini pope Urban VIII.
Like many other buildings of the period, it was made from Colosseum stone. The main hall is breathtaking, with its glorification of
the papacy on its ceiling two storeys high. The picture gallery, now
known as the **National Gallery of Ancient Art**, contains a Canaletto,
an El Greco, Holbein's *Henry VIII*, Caravaggio's *Judith*, and Raphael's
beloved *Fornarina*.

A little down the hill is the **Piazza Barberini**, once a picturesque local market-place, now the hub of several traffic-congested roads and a Metro station. At its centre (if you can get there) is Bernini's famous **Triton Fountain**. Four dolphins support an enormous scallop shell, on which sits a fishtailed sea-god blowing a conch from which the water spouts.

Across the road, on the corner of Via Veneto, Bernini completed his hat-trick with a smaller **Bee Fountain** (*Fontana delle Api*) whose water falls into a shell from which bees (the Barberini heraldic emblem) are drinking.

Just up the main road from the fountain (Via Veneto) is the Capuchin church of the **Immaculate Conception**, unremarkable except for the ossuary (*vulgo* 'boneshop') approached by the right hand steps. The skulls and skeletons of thousands of one's brothers, arranged in geometrical patterns, may not be to everyone's taste, but they provide a powerful meditation on death.

> Requiem aeternam dona eis Domine
> Et lux perpetua luceat eis.

BARCACCIA Fountain
see p.118.

BARTHOLOMEW, Church of St.
see p.129.

BATHS (TERME) OF CARACALLA

A 20 minute walk due south of the Colosseum, on the Via delle Terme di Caracalla, Map H4. Open Sun and Mon 9.00-13.00, Tue to Sat 9.00-18.00 (winter 15.00). Admission charge, except for under 18's and over 60's.

The public baths (*thermae*) of ancient Rome were highly important social centres, and emperors vied with each other to provide larger and more sumptuous facilities. For their purpose was never a merely hygienic one. The vast complexes included not only baths but also shops, hairdressers, eating and meeting places, libraries, art galleries, sports grounds and gardens. A modern sports centre combined with a shopping mall would be the nearest equivalent, and explains the lavish style on which the Roman baths were built. Caracalla's were not Rome's largest, but certainly its most luxurious. Today one sees only the brick ruins, but as Caracalla designed them in 215AD they were covered in marble and mosaic, and filled with sculpture (the famous *Farnese Hercules* now in Naples was just one of dozens of fine pieces unearthed here).

Those taking a bath (men and women at different hours) would go first to the *apodypteria* or changing rooms, and then be smeared with oil before entering the humid *caldarium*, a kind of sauna heated by slaves working underground, where a *strigil* was supplied to scrape away the sweated dirt. Beyond was the *tepidarium* to allow a cooling off period. It was only then that they would go to the only pools in the place for an invigorating cold dip in the *frigidarium*. A final massage was available, by a member of the opposite sex if requested.

The spectacular ruins (Shelley wrote his *Prometheus Unbound* perched on them) are today imaginatively used as an outdoor theatre in the summer season, particularly for the performance of operas. The splendid stage area offers a scope for camels and elephants not dreamt of in La Scala or Covent Garden. Bring warm clothing if you come early or late in the season.

BATHS (TERME) OF DIOCLETIAN

> Facing the Termini Railway Station. Metro A and B. Map E4. Museum open 9.00-14.00 (Sun 13.00). Closed Mon. Admission charge, except for under 18's and over 60's.

A hundred years after Caracalla (see above), the emperor Diocletian built here the largest of Rome's public baths, with a capacity for 3,000 bathers. It occupied a square measuring 350m each side, with an apse (*exedra*) still visible in the semi-circular **Piazza del Esedra** (or **Repubblica**) at the top of the Via Nazionale. The dramatic fountain in this square was unveiled by pope Pius IX in 1870. The sportive unveiled figures were diplomatically not added until later. They look best floodlit.

In 1561, Michelangelo was commissioned to convert the ruins into a Carthusian monastery, with a church of **St Mary of the Angels** (the original *tepidarium*) to its west. His nave was eventually transformed into the transept of the even larger present church, now entered from the piazza, with Houdon's 18th century imposing statue of St Bruno, founder of the Carthusians, to welcome the visitor. The original massive granite pillars still support the 28m vault of the church and recall (better than any other Roman building) the grandeur that was Rome. A Domenichino *Martyrdom of St Sebastian* in the right tribune is worth seeing.

> Ave Maria, gratia plena, Dominus tecum;
> benedicta tu in mulieribus,
> et benedictus fructus ventris tui, Jesus.

Sancta Maria, mater Dei,
ora pro nobis peccatoribus,
nunc et in hora mortis nostrae. Amen.

Our Father in heaven,
we join the angel in greeting Mary.
She is the beginning of the good news
that Jesus comes to us.
You chose her and loved her
to show us how chosen and loved all of us are.

How blessed is the mother who gave birth to that child,
and how blessed is the child she gave birth to,
through whom we know exactly what you are like.
We hold her hand as we ask you to accept us,
now, and at the testing time of our death.
We mean this.

On leaving the church, turn left and skirt the building to the entrance of the **National Museum** which has been built around the cloisters of the one time monastery to house over 100,000 classical treasures found in and around Rome. It is the finest museum of it kind, and includes the famous *Daughter of Niobe*, *Maid of Anzio*, *Gaul and his Wife*, and *Ludovisi Throne*. In the Early Christian Section, Gallery 39 has a graffito of a crucified figure with an ass's head, with the words 'Alexamenos worships his God', reminiscent of the Beatitudes (see below). The exhibits are well labelled, but because of restoration work are not always on view. Some of them are currently (1993) being transferred to a new annex in the Palazzo Massimo, closer to the Station.

> *Matthew 5: 11-12*: Blessed are you when men revile you [lit. make an ass of you] and persecute you and utter all kinds of evil against you falsely on my account. Rejoice and be glad, for your reward is great in heaven.

BEE FOUNTAIN
see p.36.

BOCCA DELLA VERITÀ
see p.89.

BORGHESE GARDENS
see p.139.

BORGO

Map E1-2.

The whole area between the Castel S. Angelo (see p.44) and St Peter's (see p.109) is known as **The Borgo**, and many of its streets bear that name. The word is an italianisation of the Saxon *burgh* or borough, and refers to the Saxon colony which established itself here from the 7th century onwards, to provide a home from home for pilgrims coming to visit St Peter's, long before the founding of the hospice across the river which eventually became the English College (see p.63). Other Teuton colonies followed (Lombards, Franks, etc), but the Saxons were the first to come here. They showed their devotion to St Peter not only by building numerous churches of that name back in Saxon Britain (Westminster Abbey among the first), but by sending their kings to pay homage to the Vicar of Peter, such as Canute and Alfred (whose father is said to have introduced the tax called *Peter's Pence*, eventually abolished by Henry VIII). The name 'Saxon' is still remembered in the Tiber embankment here called *Lungotevere in Sassia*, and in the hospital of *S. Spirito in Sassia*, covering part of the original settlement.

CAFFÈ GRECO
see p.118.

CAIUS CESTIUS, Tomb of.

Metro B, Piramide. Map H3.

One of Rome's most distinctive features, because so unexpected, is the white marble 37m high **Pyramid** erected just outside the Gate of St Paul. It is the tomb of a Roman magistrate, buried in 12BC, at a time when Egyptian architecture was in vogue.

Behind it lies the **Protestant Cemetery**, a noble Roman acknowledgement that non-Catholics may prefer to remain separate. The entrance is in the Via Caio Cestio 6, and it is open every day except Wed from 8.00-11.30 and 15.30-17.30. In the main part of the cemetery, shaded by cypresses, may be found the graves of the *Coral Island* author Ballantyne, and (under a tower on the wall) of the poet Shelley who died in 1822 aged 30. Much nearer to the pyramid lies the poet Keats, 1821, aged 26. Shelley wrote his *Adonais* to lament this death.

Only a short distance away from this cemetery are the graves of 400 British soldiers who died in and around Rome in the last days of World War II.

Trelawny: Nothing of him that doth fade,
But doth suffer a sea change
Into something rich and strange.

(Epitaph to Shelley)

Keats: Here lies one whose name was writ in water.

(Epitaph for his own tomb)

Shelley: It might make one in love with death
to think that one should be buried in so sweet a place.

Shelley: Flowers, ruins, statues, music, words, are weak
The glory they transfuse with fitting truth to speak.

(Adonais)

CALLISTUS, Catacomb of St.

see p.48.

CAMPIDOGLIO (Capitol)

see p.42.

CAMPO DEI FIORI

Map F2.

The colourful Campo dei Fiori lies just south of the Corso Vittorio Emmanuele, halfway along its length. Once a place of public executions, it is now a morning market for food and flowers (*fiori*). There are many fine eating places in the square and in the streets leading off, but read the displayed prices first.

In the centre of the square stands the sombre statue of Giordano Bruno, the Dominican monk burnt here by the 'Holy' Inquisition in 1600 for stating, sixteen years before Galileo, that the Copernican discovery that the earth went round the sun, and not *vice versa*, required a re-interpretation of the first chapter of Genesis. The statue was boldly erected in 1889 by an anti-clerical Italian Government, and the plinth adds the names of Wyclif and John Hus as also calling for a firm purpose of amendment.

G. Bruno: The Godhead is not to be sought far away from us. We have it within ourselves. In the same way, those who live in other worlds ought not to seek God in our world, since he is already in their world, and in them.

In the semi-circular Vicolo di Grotta Pinta just east of the Campo, one can still trace the outline of the **Theatre of Pompey**, seating 17,000, built while Caesar was invading Britain in 55BC.

Caesar was assassinated here in 44BC. Never having made the pilgrimage to Rome, Shakespeare got it wrong.

Just to the southeast, in the Piazza Capo di Ferro, is the 17th century **Palazzo Spada**, its façade and courtyard generously decorated with stucco and statues, and shining brighter than ever since a recent spring-clean. The courtyard offers a fascinating optical illusion: an archway on the left opens onto a colonnade at the end of which stands an imposing statue. In fact, the colonnade is only 10m long, and the statue only 60cm high. The brilliant foreshortening used to be attributed to Borromini, but is now thought to be the work of an Augustinian monk with a sense of humour.

The picture gallery in the palace has a Breughel, a del Sarto and several Titians, and is well worth a visit. (Admission charge except for under 18's and over 60's. Open daily 9.00-14.00).

CAMPUS MARTIUS (Campo Marzio)

Map EF2

'The field of (the war-god) Mars' was the Roman name given to the semi-circular plain between the Tiber and the hills to the east. It was the hills that were first settled, but this low-lying area became residential from the time of Augustus, who provided it with temples, baths, theatres and arenas, and was himself buried there (see p.97). Many of these fine buildings were destroyed by the Vandal and Gothic invasions of the 5th and 6th centuries, and when the aqueducts were cut, the remaining population of Rome retired to this loop of the river. This is mediæval Rome, as picturesque and fascinating as the corresponding loop of Trastevere to the south.

Strabo 7BC: The size of this plain is amazing. It is big enough to accommodate both horse and chariot races in the circus, and the crowds who gather for ball games in the gymnasia. There is grass everywhere, green all the year round, surrounded by buildings and hills that reach right down to the river. The whole scenery is such that you can hardly tear yourself away.

CANCELLERIA PALACE

Off the Corso Vittorio Emmanuele, near Campo dei Fiori. Map F2.

This majestic renaissance palace, one of the finest in Rome, was built of Colosseum stone about 1500AD. It became – and remains – the papal chancery office, and is legally part of the Vatican State. It boasts a salon which was painted by Vasari in 1546 in only a hundred days. Michelangelo's comment was, 'It shows'. The palace is not open to the public, though they are allowed to step into the courtyard to admire its noble simplicity. Off the courtyard, but with its own entrance, is one of Rome's oldest churches, built in the 4th century in honour of the Roman martyr St Lawrence (see p.84), by the rather ruthless pope who commissioned St Jerome to translate the Bible into the 'vulgar tongue', ie Latin. In memory of this pope, Damasus, the church is known as **S. Lorenzo in Damaso**. It was updated by Bramante when he completed the palace.

CAPITOL (Campidoglio)

Map F3, see plan below.

All the laws by which Rome once governed the whole civilised world were made on this small hill, the religious and political centre of ancient Rome. It remains today the meeting place of the city Senate, which continues to use the acronym which made it famous in classical times – SPQR, The Senate and People of Rome. Though it is no longer the finishing point of the triumphal processions which once wound their way up the hill from the Via Sacra in the Forum below, it is still here that heads of State are received and official receptions held.

The approach is by a noble ceremonial ramp (1), presided over by classical statues of the twin deities Castor and Pollux, guardians

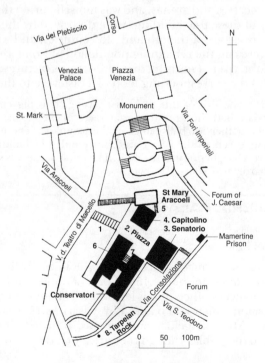

of the city. Halfway up, two cages (which until recently contained two live wolf dogs) recall the legendary forefathers of Rome, Romulus and Remus, the abandoned twins who were suckled by a she-wolf. The ramp opens onto a **Piazza** (2) of great dignity, designed by Michelangelo in the 16th century. To provide a focal point, he brought here the exquisite equestrian statue of the 2nd century philisopher-emperor Marcus Arelius, long mistakenly taken to be a statue of Constantine, and up till then displayed by the Lateran basilica where he was thought to have been baptised. Over the centuries, the gilt-bronze statue has suffered so badly from pollution that it has recently been removed into the adjacent museum, leaving only a plinth to mark the spot. There is talk of a replica to take its place.

The towered building ahead is Rome's City Hall, the **Palazzo Senatorio** (3), approached by a handsome double staircase which winds its way round a fountain graced by classical statues of Minerva, the Tiber and the Nile. This building is not open to the public, but the two palaces either side of it are museums, the first ever made available to the public (1773). They are open 9.00-13.30, plus Tues 17.00-20.00, and Sat in summer (when the piazza is floodlit) 20.00 -23.00. Closed Mon. Admission charge – a single ticket for both. Last Sunday of the month free.

The palace to the left is the **Museo Capitolino** (4), and contains an extensive range of classical sculpture, including now the equestrian statue of *Marcus Aurelius* mentioned above. Other famous pieces are the *Capitoline Venus* and the *Dying Gaul*, both Roman copies of Greek originals. There is a gallery of heads of Roman emperors, all except Augustus rather grimly Victorian, and another of busts of philosophers. In the main courtyard is the reclining *Marforio*, with whom Pasquino used to exchange witticisms (see p.107). Behind the building, a short flight of steps (5) provides easy access to the side door of the **Aracoeli**, once the temple of Juno 'Queen of Heaven' (see p.87).

Juno's consort Jupiter, the 'Father God', had his temple on the eminence now crowned by the **Conservatori Palace** (6), in part of which the city councillors meet. The museum entrance leads into a courtyard which displays the fragments of the colossal statue of Constantine (the head alone is 2.5m high) which once dominated the Basilica of Maxentius (see p.70). Inside, the most famous exhibits are a piece of the wall of the 6th century BC temple of Jupiter, the Etruscan *Capitoline Wolf* of the same antiquity (the suckling infants are a 16th century addition), the graceful *Esquiline Venus*, and the 1st century BC *Boy with a Thorn*. A fine picture gallery displays works by Caravaggio, Rubens, Tintoretto, Titian, Velàsquez and Vermeer.

Towards the far end of this palace, there is an archway (7) through the building which emerges in a lane behind. This leads shortly to the promontory overlooking the Forum known as the **Tarpeian Rock** (8). It is named after a Roman lady of the 7th century BC who offered to betray this citadel to the invading Sabines if they rewarded her with what they wore on their arms. They did: they crushed her to death with their shields. From then, all traitors were hurled onto the Forum below from this rock, forever branded with Tarpeia's name.

Marcus Aurelius:
Whatever anyone else does or says, my only duty is to do good.
Our life is what our thoughts make it.
Nothing will ever happen to you that Nature hasn't enabled you to bear.
To be perfect, live out each day as if it's your last, with no rush, no laziness, no play-acting.
If anyone wrongs you, ask yourself why he did it. When you known this, you won't be surprised or angry, only sorry for him.

(Meditations)

CARCER MAMERTINUS
see p.86.

CARLO, San
see p.51.

CASTEL S. ANGELO

Map E2. Usually open 9.00-13.00 only, except Mon 14.00-19.00. Bar, restaurant and toilets. Admission charge, except for under 18's and over 60's.

The Puccini opera *Tosca*, which begins in S. Andrea della Valle (see p.31), finishes in this spectacular place, with the heroine throwing herself off the ramparts. But it did not begin life as a fairy tale castle. It was originally built in 135AD by the emperor Hadrian (the same who built 'Hadrian's Wall' in England) as a successor and rival to the Mausoleum of Augustus (see p.97). On a square plinth he erected a massive cylinder of stone, 64m in diameter and 20m high, decorated with statues. Both plinth and cylinder were faced with white marble. A spiral corridor led to the centre of this structure where the family tomb was placed, covered with a porphyry lid which was illuminated daily by the midday sun through a hole in the ceiling. Crowning the whole structure was an inverted cone of soil,

planted with cypress trees, and topped by a statue of the sun god in his chariot, the horses of which now grace St Mark's Square in Venice.

During the barbarian invasions of the 5th century, the topsoil was removed in order to turn the whole structure into a fortress, a strategic point in Rome's wall defences. It was during this time that pope Gregory the Great had his vision of an angel on the fortress sheathing his sword and marking the end of the Great Plague in 590AD. A stone statue of this vision was erected on the roof (hence the present name), later to be replaced by a bronze.

From the 14th century onwards, the fortress was appropriated by the popes, who found it a useful bolt-hole when the Vatican was threatened, and built the raised passageway which still links the two. It was the popes too who added the present outworks and corner bastions. From 1870, under the monarchy, the whole complex became a garrison and prison. Since 1901 it has been a museum.

The visit begins up a gentle ramp, which passes over the tomb-chamber where Hadrian's touching poem to his soul is displayed (see below). Stairs then lead up to the main courtyard, where cannons (made from Pantheon bronze see p.105), piles of stone cannon balls and dungeon trap doors remind us of past sieges. In the rooms leading off here (or up short flights to mezzanine floors) may be found displays of armoury; store rooms (22,000 litres of oil could be stored in siege times); prison cells (Giordano Bruno, Benvenuto Cellini and Beatrice Cenci were held here); a library; mediæval strongboxes for Vatican treasures; chapels, one designed by Michelangelo; the gorgeous papal apartments with their lavish bedrooms and a centrally heated bathroom surprisingly explicit in its decoration; and a restaurant and bar. The final flight of steps leads to the upper terrace from which the angel surveys the whole of Rome.

The bridge which links the Castel with the city is also the work of Hadrian, and his central arches are still intact. It is now decorated with ten angels bearing instruments of the Passion. They were designed by Bernini, though the only two he himself carved finished up in a back street in Rome (see p.31).

Emperor Hadrian:	*T.S.Jerome*:
Animula, vagula, blandula,	Genial, little, vagrant sprite,
hospes comesque corporis,	long my body's friend and guest,
quae nunc abibis in loca,	to what place is now thy flight?
pallidula, rigida, nudula,	Pallid, stark and naked quite,
nec ut soles dabis jocos?	stripped henceforth of joke and jest.
(Epitaph)	*(Roman Memories)*

CASTEL GANDOLFO
see p.142.

CATACOMBS

Access to the three catacombs in the south is by bus 118 from the Lateran or the Colosseum. The two northern catacombs can be reached by buses from outside Termini Station.

The 'Church of the catacombs' is a phrase we have all grown up with. It conjures up the image of a persecuted minority living in bolt-holes, keeping a low profile, and ready to go underground at the first sign of trouble. It is a phrase frequently in use when we are urged to be bold in professing our faith: 'We are no longer the Church of the catacombs'.

In actual fact the Roman catacombs were never hiding holes for Christians. There was no secrecy about them because they were simply the official cemeteries in which Christians, among others, buried their dead outside the city walls, as the law required. But land was expensive, especially for those like Christians and Jews who preferred burial to cremation. So when they ran out of room, they simply extended their plots vertically instead of horizontally. The result was a labyrinth of narrow corridors carved out of the soft *tufa* rock, each lined up to the ceiling on either side with *loculi* or niches in which the bodies of the dead were placed and sealed with a slab of terracotta or marble. Occasionally, larger areas were excavated to allow the faithful to gather in order to commemorate the anniversary of their loved ones, especially those that had been martyred. But it was (and continues to be) absurd to imagine that Christians ever lived there.

There are fifty or more catacombs surrounding Rome, some of them six levels deep. Put end to end, the galleries carved out by the ancient miners would stretch 1,000km. It is estimated that up to six million Christians were buried there, 'like a troopship in the dark', says H.V.Morton, 'with its rows of bunks, their occupants sleeping, confidently awaiting the light of a new day'. Some of the slabs are inscribed with a name or a Christian symbol (fish, anchor, lamb, ship, IXΘYC), and occasionally the confident words *In Pace* or *Vivas in Deo* (In peace, May you live in God), contrasting interestingly with the usual pagan inscription *Vale* (Goodbye). The tombs of the wealthy are more elaborately decorated with paintings and stucco.

When Constantine put an end to 300 years of persecution in the 4th century, the Christian catacombs enjoyed a period of great popularity with pilgrims to Rome. But during the invasions of the 'dark ages', when tombs were regularly plundered in search of treasure, many of the relics were transferred to safety within Rome's walls (see pp.106 & 120). As a result, the catacombs were no longer

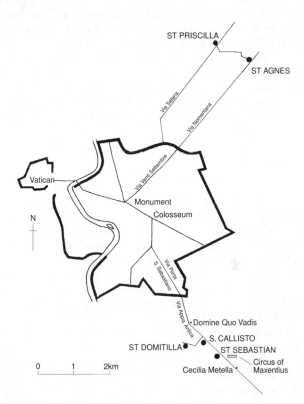

visited (apart from those of St Sebastian, see below), and even their sites were forgotten until an explorer of the 16th century stumbled across them again. Much manual and scholarly work has been done on them since, especially under the influence of the 19th century archæologist De Rossi.

Most of the catacombs are open to visitors, but never without a local guide. Even these, of course, can lose their way in these networks of corridors and floors. An enthusiastic guide once offered to take me to see a little known Hebrew inscription. It was not far away, but it took him a full hour and a half to find his way back. I must have told the story to a group very dramatically, because at the end I was asked, 'Did you get out?'

Each of the catacombs below is open from 8.30-12.00, and from 14.30-17.00, but please note the day on which it is closed. There is an admission charge to each. The local guide will provide plenty of details. Here only a simple outline is offered.

Callisto

Via Appia, closed Wed.

This is the largest of the Christian catacombs and the best preserved. It is lovingly tended by the Salesian Fathers. They estimate that 170,000 Christians were buried in the 20km of galleries that have so far been explored. The entrance leads into a noble subterranean church, where many of the persecuted 3rd century popes were buried, as a great number of the devout *graffiti* of the 4th-6th century testify. Close by was the tomb of St Cecilia, and a copy of the Maderna statue (see p.50) has been placed under the altar.

Sebastian

Via Appia, closed Thurs.

Less than a kilometre further down the Via Appia lies the only catacomb that never sank into oblivion, now served by the Franciscan Fathers. St Sebastian's has always been visited by pilgrims without interruption, to become one of the traditional Seven Churches of Rome (see p.174). In fact the word 'catacomb', eventually applied to all the others, came from this 2nd century site, which was always described as being on the Via Appia *kata kumbas* ('near the dip in the road'). St Philip Neri, founder of the Oratorians, often spent the night in prayer here.

Its importance derives from the fact that the bodies of Sts Peter and Paul, originally buried just outside the Roman walls, were thought to be safer in this popular place, and were temporarily transferred here in the 3rd century. Numerous inscriptions of that date, in Greek and Latin, appeal for the prayers of the apostles.

The winding and intersecting galleries descend to four levels. A fine underground church commemorates St Sebastian, a captain in the Roman army martyred in the 3rd century. The church now above ground level has retained some ancient columns, but is largely a baroque restoration.

Domitilla

Via Ardeatina, closed Tues.

Close to these two famous sites, on a side road, are the catacombs of St Domitilla, a relative of the emperor Vespasian, who invited Christians to use her family tomb. There are some impressive and well preserved wall paintings in these galleries, which lead to the fine underground church of Sts Nereus and Achilles, converted soldiers like Sebastian.

Agnes

Via Nomentana 349, closed on holy days.

The young virgin martyr Agnes (see p.100) was buried 2km north of the city in a tomb commissioned by the emperor Constantine himself. The catacomb was extended to a depth of three storeys, and the galleries stretch for 7km. Above ground a fine basilica was later constructed in the 7th century, with a richly decorated ceiling and a glorious mosaic apse. It is here that flower-bedecked lambs (*agnus*) are blessed each 21st January, later to be shorn for the twelve *pallia* (patterned neckbands) woven each year for new archbishops by the nuns of St Cecilia in Trastevere (see p.50).

Nearby, further up the hill, is the delightful little round church of **St Constantia** (S. Constanza), daughter of Constantine, who built the first church of St Agnes. With its 4th century mosaics, it is probably the oldest in Rome, and some think the most beautiful.

Priscilla

Via Salaria 430, closed Mon.

Only 700m from St Agnes, but on another road running north from Rome, lies the catacomb of the 1st century martyr S. Priscilla, noted for its fine 2nd century frescoes, particularly of the three Magi on the portico of its Greek chapel, and of Isaiah's 'prophecy' of the virgin birth of Jesus. It was also here that the mysterious tomb of a 14-year old girl was found in 1802. Its inscription LUMENA PAX TE CUM FI, was reconstructed into the name Philomena, and the Curé d'Ars enthusiastically spread her veneration. Sadly, it was later discovered that the stone slab came from another unknown tomb. The Greek word *philoumena* means no more than 'Beloved'.

Isaiah 7: 14:
The Lord himself will give you a sign.
Behold, a young woman shall conceive
and bear a son,
and shall call his name Immanuel,
that is, God with us.

Mediæval graffito:
There is light in this darkness;
there is music in these tombs.

F.W.Faber:
Faith of our Fathers, living still
in spite of dungeon, fire and sword:
oh how our hearts beat high with joy
whene'er we hear that glorious word!
Faith of our Fathers! Holy Faith!
We will be true to thee till death.

T.S.Eliot:
Why should men love the Church? Why should they love her laws?
She tells them of Life and Death, and of all that they would forget.
She is tender where they would be hard, and hard where they like
    to be soft.
She tells them of Evil and Sin, and other unpleasant facts.
They constantly try to escape
From the darkness outside and within
By dreaming of systems so perfect that no one will need to be good.
But the man that is will shadow the man that pretends to be.
And the Son of Man was not crucified once for all,
The blood of the Martyrs not shed once for all,
The lives of the Saints not given once for all:
But the Son of Man is crucified always
And there shall be Martyrs and Saints. (*Rock VI*, Faber & Faber)

CECILIA, Church of St.

Via S. Cecilia. Map G2.

In the warren of lanes that is Trastevere, it is a sheer delight to enter the spacious garden courtyard of St Cecilia, at the end of which stands an early Christian church, said to be built on the site of the saint's house. The present church is an 18th century rebuilding, further restored at the end of the 19th century. It contains an apse decorated in 9th century mosaics, a fine 13th century canopy by Arnolfo di Cambio, and underneath it a 16th century recumbent figure of the saint by Maderna.

We know nothing of St Cecilia apart from the legend written about her. An aristocrat of 300AD who had heard the good news of the Gospel and become a Christian, she is said to have been condemned to death by the emperor Diocletian. When a night locked in her private *thermae* with the heat full on did not suffocate her, she was sent to be decapitated. Even so, the executioner could not totally sever her head. Buried in the catacombs, this is how she was found in 1599, when her tomb was opened, incorrupt, and head still attached. Her association with music is sadly due to a mistranslation.

Beneath the altar, Cardinal Rampolla, protector of the church, paid for the construction of a tasteful crypt which is worth visiting. It leads to the remains of a Roman house. The adjoining convent of enclosed Benedictine nuns displays the famous Cavallini fresco of the *Last Judgement* (13th century). Open to the public on Sun 11.00-12.00, and on Tues and Thurs 10.00-12.00.

The sculptor Maderna:
Behold the body of the most holy virgin Cecilia,
whom I myself saw lying incorrupt in the tomb.
In this marble I have made for you the image of that saint
in the very posture in which I saw her.

CECILIA METELLA
see p.33.

CESTIUS, CAIUS
see p.39.

CHARLES, Churches of St. (S. Carlo)

St Charles Borromeo, the 16th century archbishop of Milan and indefatigable champion of the reforms proposed by the Council of Trent, died of exhaustion at the early age of 46. Only 25 years later he was canonised, and three Roman churches were built in his honour soon after. His heart was enshrined behind the high altar of the richly decorated **S. Carlo al Corso** (Map E3), but it is Borromini's 1667 **S. Carlo alle Quattro Fontane** (Map E3) that attracts most visitors. Built on an area no larger than the base of one of the piers supporting the dome of St Peter's, the geometrical perfection of its convex and concave lines continue to fascinate the viewer.

The cross roads outside, with a fountain at each corner (*quattro fontane*), offers a vista of the Mary Major obelisk to the south east, the Quirinal obelisk to the south west, the Trinità obelisk to the north west, and the Porta Pia to the north east. But mind the traffic.

51

17th century General of the Trinitarian Fathers:
Everyone agrees that in the whole world there is no work of art that can be compared with this one, for merit, caprice, excellence or singularity.

CHIESA NUOVA
see p.96.

CHURCHES
see under name.

CIRCUS MAXIMUS

Metro B, Circo Massimo. Map G3.

In the valley south of the Palatine hill, and therefore conveniently placed for the gorgeous imperial palaces above, Rome built its Ascot as long ago as the 2nd century AD. It measured 370m by 82m, and could seat 300,000 spectators (a collapse of the cushioned seating killed over a thousand in the 2nd century, and further 13,000 in the 3rd). It was used for occasional combats with animals as the Colosseum was, but mainly for horse races (with or without chariots) in which seven laps had to be completed round the central dividing *spina* on which stood the obelisks now in the Popolo and Lateran squares. Race meetings could last for a fortnight, and they continued being held, in spite of Church prohibitions, until the 5th century. Shops and taverns were provided in the arcades that supported the structure.

The stones that were once one of the wonders of the ancient world have now been recycled, and the weed-filled stadium is deserted apart from the occasional game of knockabout football.

CLEMENT, Church of St.

Map G4. Via S. Giovanni in Laterano. Metro B, Colosseo. Open 9.00-12.00 and (except Sun), 15.30-18.00. Small admission charge to the excavations (*scavi*).

Those interested in tracing the historical development of this remarkable place would do well to visit the ground-level church last (it is the third built here), and begin with the first one, two floors down. Entrance is off the present right aisle.

After two flights of stairs, the sound of water from underground streams assures us we are on ground rock, where a small first century vaulted room, with stone seats around, was built as a *mithraeum*. In the centre stands an altar with a carving of the god Mithras slaying a bull to release eternal life to the whole world. The cult was so popular among soldiers that it survived in the Roman army long after all religions but the Christian one were outlawed. Alongside this relic of pagan Rome is the house of a family of this same first century. Since a church was eventually built above this spot, there is (some think) reason to suppose that it was the house of St Clement, fourth in the list of bishops of Rome, who was possibly the Clement mentioned in St Paul's letter to the Christians of Philippi. If so, then Peter and Paul, in the days they spent in Rome, would have been familiar with this Christian house-church hidden in the midst of unbelievers. According to a later legend, Clement was eventually taken prisoner in Domitian's persecution, deported to the Crimea, and there drowned, an anchor tied round his neck.

In the 4th century the Christians of Rome, newly liberated by Constantine's conversion, wanted to venerate this early Christian saint, and built a basilica in his name over the Roman house. We come back upstairs to see what is left of it. Very little, since the supporting pillars of the upper church have obscured its fine lines. But the right aisle still has a beautiful portrait of a Roman lady of the period, and the left aisle a series of frescoes of legends associated with the life of Clement, dating from the 11th century (and strangely of St Alexis as well, see p.124). Further along is a shrine in honour of the Slavonic saints Cyril and Methodius, who are said to have brought the relics of St Clement to Rome from the east.

The whole of this church was destroyed in the Norman sack of Rome in 1084, leaving only a pile of stones. A few marble panels and stone columns were rescued for building the third church, to which we finally re-ascend. Smaller than the 4th century church below, but built in exactly the same style in 1108, it is a perfect example of Rome's earliest Christian basilicas, brilliant with white marble, mosaics and Cosmati pavement. The raised choir is screened off, and the altar placed under a graceful canopy, with the sunken tomb of St Clement in front of it. Behind, the mosaic apse glows gold, with the crucified Christ giving life to the world, and deer drinking from the life-giving waters flowing from the cross. A recently restored chapel at the rear of the left aisle has some fine 15th century Masolino murals of the life of St Catherine of Alexandria. Beyond the west entrance to the church there is a welcoming courtyard (toilets).

The Irish Dominican Order, supporters of Bonnie Prince Charlie when he was exiled in Rome, were put in charge of this site in 1645. It is they who began the excavations a hundred years ago, removing hundreds of tons of rubble to reveal the archæological treasures beneath. They continue to receive visitors with grace and courtesy, and have a fine display of books and postcards at the entrance to the excavations.

John 7: 37-38:
Jesus proclaimed, 'If anyone thirst, let him come to me, and let him who believes in me drink. As the Scripture has said, "Out of his heart shall flow rivers of living water." '

Philippians 4: 2-4:
I entreat Evodia and I entreat Synteche to agree in the Lord. And I ask you also, Syzygus, to be a real 'partner' and help these women, for they have laboured side by side with me in the gospel, together with *Clement* and the rest of my fellow workers, whose names are in the book of life. Rejoice in the Lord always; again I will say, Rejoice.
Paul writing from prison (Rome?)

Psalm 42 (41):
Like the deer that years for running streams
so my soul is yearning for you, my God.
My soul is thirsting for God, the God of my life;
when can I enter and see the face of God?
Deep is calling on deep in the roar of waters:
your torrents and all your waves swept over me.
Why are you cast down, my soul, why groan within me?
Hope in God; I will praise him still, my saviour and my God.
(Grail version)

Roman Canon of Mass:
In union with the whole Church,
We honour Mary …
the apostles and martyrs Peter and Paul …
Linus, Cletus, *Clement* …

St Clement to the Corinthians:
Let us show kindliness to one another, in the same sweet spirit of tenderness as our Maker… Christ belongs to the lowly of heart, and not to those who would exalt themselves… The coming of our Lord Jesus Christ, the Sceptre of God's Majesty, was in no pomp of pride and haughtiness – as it could so well have been – but in self-abasement… Why must there be all this quarrelling and bad blood, these feuds and dissensions among you? Have we not all the same God and the same Christ? Is not the same Spirit of grace shed upon us all? Have we not all the same calling in Christ? Then why are we rending and tearing asunder the limbs of Christ, and foment-ing discord against our own body? Why are we so lost to all sense and reason that we have forgotten our membership of one another?… Love knows of no divisions, promotes no discord; all the works of love are done in perfect fellowship.
(written from Rome 96AD)

54

CLOACA MAXIMA
see p.89.

COLLEGIO ROMANO
see p.78.

COLONNA, Piazza

> Halfway along the Via del Corso, on the west.
> Map E3.

This central piazza is named after the column standing at the centre. 29.5m high (exactly 100 Roman feet), it was put up for the emperor Marcus Aurelius in the 2nd century AD, in imitation of the even larger one dedicated to his predecessor Trajan (see p.71). Like that, it is made of marble drums, on which has been carved a spiral relief of scenes from the emperor's campaign against the Germanic tribes on the Danube. Inside, a staircase gives access to the top, where a figure of Aurelius was replaced with a statue of St Paul by Fontana in the 16th century (St Peter is on the higher Trajan's column).

The piazza used to be a very friendly place to stroll in, but in these days it has inevitably become a car park. Just beyond to the west are the Parliament Buildings, to the south the Stock Exchange, and to the east the busy shopping street of the Via del Tritone.

COLOSSEUM

> Map FG3-4. Metro B, Colosseo. Open 9.00-16.00
> (summer to 19.00), Wed and Sun until 13.00
> only. Entrance is free, though a charge is made
> for ascending to the upper levels, except for
> under 18's and over 60's.

London's Albert Hall holds 5,000 spectators. The Colosseum held 50,000. It is no wonder that this *Flavian Amphitheatre* has been called, since the time of Bede, 'The Colossus'. Even though only a third of the original structure remains, it still stupefies visitors, especially when they see it gently illuminated by night, its dilapidation disguised.

The Colosseum is Rome's largest monument, half a kilometre in circumference and rising to a height of 57m. It was built of travertine stone faced with marble, and was erected in the last days of the emperor Vespasian, who was determined to restore to the public the land which his predecessor Nero had confiscated for an

55

artificial lake alongside his **Golden House** (see p.75). It was completed in 80AD by his son Titus, probably using gangs of Jewish captives he had brought back from his war in Palestine. The vast project continues to astonish engineers, who even today would hesitate to build such a gigantic structure on a drained marsh, and elevate it four storeys high, with 76 entrances, and enough corridors and stairways to allow access and exit within minutes. Above, 240 masts allowed a special naval corps to manoeuvre a vast awning to shelter spectators from sun or rain – and the corbels for the ropes are still visible. Below, the 86m wide arena covered a complex of passages which provided storage, changing rooms and animal cages which could be raised and lowered on pulleys and lifts as required.

The arena could be flooded for naval battles. But the usual 'entertainment' consisted of morning combats with animals (a text of 204AD records the slaughter of thirty elephants, ten elk, ten tigers, seventy lions, thirty leopards, ten hyenas, nineteen giraffes, twenty wild asses, forty wild horses, one hippopotamus and one rhinoceros); followed by an afternoon of individual or group fights between gladiators, whose performance was judged by the thumbs up (or down) of the audience. In between rounds, the auditorium was sprayed with scent to smother the smell of blood and excrement. Entertainments of these kinds could go on for days at a time: those laid down for the opening ceremony lasted for three months. Professional gladiators could make a lot of money. The animals were not on the pay roll. It is one of the miracles of history that these barbaric and grisly spectacles, which had never been questioned by anyone over hundreds of years, finally came to an end when Rome became Christian.

By the 14th century a series of earthquakes had toppled a considerable part of the structure, and its stone and marble became a convenient quarry for renaissance churches and palaces like the Farnese, Venezia and Cancelleria. The rest remained abandoned, though one pope in the 16th century did try to turn it into a wool factory. The pillaging went on till 1750 when pope Benedict XIV called a halt, naming the Colosseum a place made sacred by the blood of so many victims, many of them Christians. It was not until the last century that the present brick buttresses were erected to shore up the ruined walls.

In front of what was once the Imperial Box, a bronze cross has been erected, which still features in the regular praying of the Stations of the Cross in this place. On Good Friday afternoon, these continue to be led by the pope.

Charles Dickens:
The most impressive, the most stately, the most solemn, grand, majestic, mournful sight conceivable.

Gladiators' greeting:
Morituri te salutamus.   Condemned to die, we salute you.

Under this cross,
symbol of man's ceaseless inhumanity to man,
we bring before God
not only the passion and death of Jesus,
but all the crucifixions that took place here,
where so many of our Christian brothers and sisters,
and countless thousands of others,
were mindlessly massacred
to provide an afternoon's entertainment.

We bring before God
not only that cruel world of yesterday,
but also the anguished world of today,
where the shadow of the cross continues to fall
on so many of the poor banished children of Eve.

We remember the victims of natural disasters,
and the victims of the wars and persecution and violence
that continue to plague our sad world.
We remember the endless processions
of refugees thrown out of their homes,
and all the victims of discrimination and humiliation
because of their race or colour or sex.
We remember the growing queues of the unemployed,
and all those who are exploited by the greed of others,
so that they fall deeper and deeper
into the poverty trap.

And we remember not only
these public tragedies in our suffering world,
but also the private ones:

those whose lives are empty or full of disappointment,
those whose marriages have broken down,
those who have been bereaved of parents,
or partners, or children,
the handicapped and those who are sick in body or in mind,
those whose sickness is incurable, or who are in pain,
those who are afraid to die,
and those who can't wait to die.

God our loving Father,
we are told that Christ will be in agony
till the end of time.
Our heart goes out
to these crucified brothers and sisters of his.
Assure us once again that you are as close to them
as you were to Jesus,
even when they feel you have forsaken them.

Close to the old Colosseum, and one of its outstanding features, was a colossal gilded statue of the Sun-god, 30m high. Nero had it made to grace the entrance to his **Golden House** (see p.75), and ensured that it bore his own features. To move it down the hill required a team of 24 elephants, and the face was changed as emperor succeeded emperor. Since oaths of loyalty had to be sworn here, the statue also went with the coming of Christianity.

Daniel 2: 31-36:
You have had a vision, Your Majesty; this is what you saw: a statue, a great statue of extreme brightness, stood before you, terrible to see. The head of this statue was of fine gold, its chest and arms were of silver, its belly and thighs of bronze, its legs of iron, its feet part iron, part clay. While you were gazing, a stone broke away, untouched by any hand, and struck the statue, struck its feet of iron and clay and shattered them. Then, iron and clay, bronze, silver and gold, all broke into pieces as fine as chaff on the threshing-floor in the summer. The wind blew them away, leaving not a trace behind. And the stone that had struck the statue grew into a great mountain, filling the whole world.

(NJB)

CONSERVATORI MUSEUM
see p.43.

CONSTANTINE'S ARCH
see p.34.

CONSTANTIA, Church of St. (Costanza)
see p.49.

CORSO

The word *corso* means a racecourse. It was originally used of Rome's main north-south artery running 2km from the northern Flaminian Gate (**del Popolo**, see p.94) to the Forum, down which races were run at Carnival times. Its official name is **Corso Umberto** or **Via del Corso**, but it is usually referred to as **The (il) Corso**. It has some magnificent 17th and 18th century façades, and remains one of Rome's busiest shopping streets. Map D2-F3.

The other **Corso** (with which it may easily be confused) is officially entitled **Corso Vittorio Emmanuele**, after Italy's first king. It is a much more recent road, constructed only since 1876, and ploughing through the densest quarter of old Rome to provide access to the Vatican. It also gives access to some of Rome's most important sites. Map F3-E2.

COSMAS AND DAMIAN, Church of Sts.

Map F3. Entrance in Via dei Fori Imperiali.

Built over one of the ruined Forum temples, but now accessible only from outside, the Church of Sts Cosmas and Damian was erected in the 6th century in memory of two brothers, both doctors, martyred in Syria in the persecutions of the 3rd century. Their cult spread throughout the Roman Empire, to the extent that they have ever since been invoked (together with St Luke) as patrons of physicians and surgeons. The church itself was remodelled in the 17th century (see the fine wooden ceiling), but the mosaics above the altar remain as they were set in the 6th century, and are among the best in Rome. On the arch, the Lamb (Christ) breaks the seven seals to reveal the hidden meaning of all our history. In the apse, Sts Peter and Paul gently introduce Cosmas and Damian to the glorious Christ. Pope Felix IV, builder of the church, looks on with approval, but worried. The church also has a beautiful and rare early painting of the Cross, on which Christ is not dead but gloriously alive (in a chapel in the right aisle). The church is cared for by Franciscans.

In the cloisters, a chapel has on permanent display a 17th century Neapolitan Christmas Crib (*Presepio*). It is the largest of all the Roman cribs, which are otherwise only brought out in December. In terracotta and carved wood, every possible aspect of Italian country life is depicted, to the extent that you have to search for the birth of Christ in the midst of it all. Isn't that true to life?

Roman Canon of Mass:
In union with the whole Church, we honour Mary... the apostles and martyrs... John and Paul, *Cosmas and Damian*, and all the saints.

Revelation 5: 2-12:
I saw a strong angel proclaiming with a loud voice, 'Who is worthy to open the scroll and break its seals?' And no one in heaven or on earth or under the earth was able to open the scroll or to look into it, and I wept much... Then one of the elders said to me 'Weep not... the Root of David has conquered, so that he can open the scroll and its seven seals... I saw a Lamb standing, as though it had been slain... and he went and took the scroll from the right hand of him who was seated on the throne. And when he had taken the scroll... they sang a new song, saying, 'Worthy is the Lamb who was slain, to receive power and wealth and wisdom and might and honour and glory and blessing!'

CROSS, Church of the Holy. (Santa Croce)

Piazza S. Croce, at the end of the Via S. Croce.
Map G5.

This church, one of the traditional 'Seven' (see p.174), has been accorded the title 'In Jerusalem' because Constantine's mother Helena, whose palace adjoined, went to Jerusalem to bring back shiploads of soil to form its foundation in the 4th century AD. She also claimed to have brought back a piece of Christ's cross, thorns from his crown, one of the nails, the INRI title, and the crossbeam of the Good Thief. These are exhibited in the chapel at the altar end of the left aisle.

Little of Helena's church survives, the present structure being 12th and 15th century (apse frescoes and crypt mosaics), thoroughly 'rococoed' in the 18th century. It is served by the Cistercians, with whom John Henry Newman stayed on a visit to Rome.

J.H. Newman:
O generous love! that he who smote
in man for man the foe,
the double agony in man
for man should undergo;
and in the garden secretly,
and on the Cross on high,
should teach his brethren, and inspire
to suffer and to die.

Isaac Watts: When I survey the wondrous Cross
on which the Prince of Glory died,
my richest gain I count but loss,
and pour contempt on all my pride.

John Donne:
We thinke that Paradise and Calvarie,
Christ's Crosse, and Adam's tree, stood in one place;
looke, Lord, and finde both Adams met in me;
as the first Adam's sweat surrounds my face,
may the last Adam's blood my soule embrace.

Venantius Fortunatus:
Faithful Cross! Above all other,
one and only noble Tree!
None in foliage, none in blossom,
none in fruit thy peer may be.
Beauteous wood and radiant iron!
Goodly weight is hung on thee!   (*trsl. J.M.Neale*)

Joseph Plunkett:
I see his blood upon the rose,
and in the stars the glory of his eyes.
His body gleams amid eternal snows,
his tears fall from the skies.

I see his face in every flower.
The thunder and the singing of the birds
are but his voice; and carven by his power,
rocks are his written words.

All pathways by his feet are worn.
His strong heart stirs the everbeating sea.
His crown of thorns is twined with every thorn.
His cross is every tree.

DOMINE QUO VADIS, Church of.
See plan on p.47.

Half way on the Via Appia Antica, the road south out of Rome
leading to the catacombs, on the left stands the little baroque
church of **Domine Quo Vadis.** It commemorates the story told in
the apocryphal *Acts of Peter* that Peter, fleeing Nero's persecution of
Christians in the Rome, met Christ coming the other way, and when
he asked, *'Domine, quo vadis?'* (Lord, where are you going?), received the reply, 'To Rome, to be crucified again'. This was enough,
says the legend, to turn Peter's steps round. He was himself
crucified, head down, in the year 64AD. Christ's 'footprint' is shown
in the church, rather as in the church of the Ascension in Jerusalem.

Perhaps it is a silent commentary on the legend that not very far
away, on the Via Ardeatina, are the **Ardeatine Caves** where 335
random Italians were machine-gunned by the German occupation
army in 1944, in reprisal for the death of 32 soldiers killed by a
resistance bomb.

Luke 14: 27:
Whoever does not bear his own cross and come after me, cannot be my
disciple.

B. Pascal:
Christ will be in agony until the end of the world.

St Patrick's Breastplate:
Christ be with me, Christ within me,
Christ behind me, Christ before me,
Christ beside me, Christ to win me,
Christ to comfort and restore me,
Christ beneath me, Christ above me,
Christ in quiet, Christ in danger,
Christ in hearts of all that love me,
Christ in mouth of friend or stranger.

DOMITILLA, St

see p.49.

DOMUS AUREA (Golden House)

see p.75.

DORIA-PAMPHILI PALACE

Via del Corso. Map F3.

The whole first block on the left as you go up the Corso from Piazza
Venezia is occupied by one of Rome's largest palaces (it has five
courtyards). Built in the 15th century though with a later façade, it
has belonged to a number of noble families, most recently the
Pamphili, into which the Doria family married. Much of the
building is now rented out, but the prince still lives in part of the
palace, as other princes do in theirs. After Waterloo, Napoleon's
mother was given a small apartment nearest the Piazza Venezia,
with a balcony from which she could watch the Corso races.

The rich art collection of these families is displayed in the
Galleria Doria-Pamphili. In a most elegant and opulent setting
(alone worth a visit), it contains many Poussins and Lorrains, and
more famously in Gallery 3, the Bernini bust of the Pamphili pope
Innocent X and the Velàsquez canvas of the same, thought by
Joshua Reynolds to be the finest portrait in Rome. The two are
worth comparing. Gallery 4 has examples of many of the Renaissance painters – Caravaggio, Correggio, Lippi, Raphael, Sassoferrato, Tintoretto and Titian. The entrance is behind the palace
in Piazza del Collegio Romano 1a. Open 10.00-13.00, closed Mon,
Wed and Thurs. Admission charge. There are guided tours of the
State Apartments for an extra charge.

The entrance from the Via del Corso 303 leads (4th floor) to the
recently established **Anglican Centre**, which houses the library of
the late Bishop Moorman, and promotes the study of the relation-
ship between the Roman Catholic and the Anglican Churches.
Visitors are welcome.

The Pamphili family have another fine palace (now the Brazilian embassy) in the Piazza Navona (see p.100), and a villa inside a vast park on the Janiculum Hill (see p.78).

ENGLISH COLLEGE (The Venerabile)

Via di Monserrato 45. Map F2.

A hospice for English pilgrims to Rome was set up in the Via di Monserrato by a group of English merchants in 1362. Later it took in resident students as well, whose number increased in the 16th century, when Catholic scholars were debarred from universities in England and preferred exile in Rome to Protestantism in England. In 1579 the hospice was extended, and became a college for training priests, being accorded the title 'Venerable' as the oldest existing British institution abroad. It has continued throughout its history to receive English pilgrims and guests, including in 1638 the poet John Milton. A summer villa in the Alban hills (see p.143) still caters for groups that wish to enjoy a Roman summer.

Students were required to take an oath to return to England as missionaries to an almost certain death. The response of its protomartyr, Ralph Sherwin, is still treasured by the college: 'Today rather than tomorrow'. Forty of his fellow students went to the gallows, of whom ten have been canonised and eighteen beatified. St Philip Neri, living opposite at the time, would greet these prospective martyrs on their way to study at the University with the words, 'Salvete, flores martyrum'. The college chapel contains a fine 1580 painting of the Trinity by Durante Alberti, before which St Thomas of Canterbury and St Edmund Martyr kneel in adoration. It was before this painting that students sang a *Te Deum* when they heard that one of their colleagues had died for his Catholic faith.

In the pleasant little garden at the end of the entrance corridor are some remains of the College of the Martyrs, flanked by a swimming pool installed and inaugurated by Cardinal Hinsley when he was rector. It was his influence, and later that of his successor Cardinal Godfrey, which ensured that a great number of English Catholic bishops did their studies here. It says much for the spirit of the college that while the 16th century students thought of themselves as exiles in Rome, their successors in 1940-46 (when the war years were spent in England) thought of themselves as exiles in England.

Bl. William Hart:
Most Dear and Loving Mother,
Seeing that by the severity of the laws, by the wickedness of our times, and by God's holy ordinance and appointment, my days in this life are cut off, of duty and conscience I am bound (being far from you in body, but in spirit very near you) not only to crave your daily blessing, but also to write these few words unto you...

I had meant this spring to have seen you if God had granted me my health and liberty; but now never shall I see you, or any of yours, in this life again; trusting yet in heaven to meet you, to see you, and to live everlastingly with you. Alas! Sweet Mother, why do you weep? Why do you lament? Why do you take so heavily my honourable death? Know you not that we are born once to die, and that always in this life we may not live?...

But perhaps you will say, I weep not so much for your death as I do for that you are hanged, drawn and quartered. My sweet mother, it is the favourablest, honourablest, and happiest death that ever could have chanced to me.

I die not for knavery, but for verity; I die not for treason, but for religion; I die not for any ill demeanour or offence committed, but only for my faith, for my conscience, for my priesthood, for my blessed Saviour Jesus Christ; and, to tell you truth, if I had ten thousand lives, I am bound to lose them all rather than to break my faith, to lose my soul, to offend my God.

We are not made to eat, drink, sleep, to go bravely, to feed daintily, to live in this wretched vale continually; but to serve God, to please God, to fear God, and to keep his commandments; which when we cannot be suffered to do, then rather must we choose to lose our lives than to desire our lives...

(From a letter to his mother, 10 March 1583)

ESEDRA, Piazza del.

see p.37.

E.U.R.

Metro B terminus. See reverse of pocket map.

E.U.R. is the Italian acronym for the *Universal Exhibition of Rome* which Mussolini was planning to hold here in 1942. World War II prevented this taking place, but a satellite town was eventually built on the site, halfway between Rome and the sea, and many government offices have emigrated there from the city. It has also given many artists the opportunity to show their paces, and some superb examples of modern architecture have been erected, most excitingly the Sports Palace. A number of museums have also chosen to exhibit here rather than in Rome, the most outstanding being the **Museum of Roman Civilisation** (Piazza G. Agnelli 10) with its enormous scale model of 3rd century Rome. Those who have trudged faithfully around the remains of the Roman Empire in the city will be delighted to find it finally and painlessly making sense before their eyes. Open 9.00-13.30 (Tues and Thurs also 15.00-18.00). Closed Mon. Admission charge. But check first that it is open (Tel: 06 592 6135).

EXCURSIONS

see p.141.

FARNESE GARDENS (Orti Farnesiani)

see p.104.

FARNESE PALACE

Near the Campo dei Fiori. Map F2.

This palace, one of the most elegant in Rome and a Renaissance masterpiece, was built during the reign of Henry VIII in England. The Farnese family was fortunate not only in having a quarry to hand (papal permission was given to take as much stone from the Colosseum as could be removed in a day, and a hired gang of 4,000 showed what could be done), but in getting Michelangelo to agree to act as one of the architects. The three storeys, of contrasting design, form a magnificent harmony, seen to perfection when the place is floodlit. Even without paying a formal visit, it is worth walking through the barrel vaulted entrance (if the security guards allow) to view the courtyard inside. Long used as a French Embassy, the palace has since 1874 been the home of the French ambassador, who pays a rent of one lira every 99 years. Its rooms are therefore on view for only half a day a week, by previous arrangement. They are worth seeing, especially the first floor gallery, two storeys high, with its brilliant and riotous 16th century frescoes by Caracci, who died of drinking away his sorrow over the miserable paypacket he received.

The generous piazza in front has two monumental fountains, granite baths borrowed from the Baths of Caracalla (see p.36), surmounted by *fleurs de lys*. The rear of the building stretches back the whole block as far as the Tiber, over which Michelangelo planned to build a private bridge to link with the garden villa on the other side, but he got no further than putting up an arch over the Via Giulia.

The sumptuous villa is known as the little Farnese, the **Farnesina**, and was built for entertaining guests in a lavish garden setting. They would be served food, we are told, on gold and silver dishes which were afterwards thrown into the river (an underwater net kept expenses down). The open-air casino from which they were served (now glazed in) was decorated throughout with frescoes of classical scenes by Raphael and his pupils Sodoma and Giulio Romano. Raphael's *Galatea*, carried on waves in a shell surrounded by nymphs and cupids, is alone worth a visit. (Open from the Via della Lungara from 9.00-13.00, Tues 15.00-17.50 as well. Closed in August. Admission charge).

FARNESINA

see p.65.

FLAMINIAN GATE (Porta Flaminia)

see p.94.

FORUM

Map F3. Entrances in the Via dei Fori Imperiali and the Via S. Gregorio. Open 9.00 till 18.00 (winter till 16.00), Sundays 9.00-13.00. Closed Tues in winter. Admission charge (under 18's and over 60's are free) allows access to the Palatine as well. Bookshop and toilets at entrances.

Everyone who comes to Rome goes to the Forum. This hub of the Roman Empire is a 'must' on the sightseer's list. Most people go away disappointed. These weedgrown acres, littered with isolated stones, tumbled columns and roofless ruins, 'like old bomb damage', writes H.V. Morton, simply baffles them, and refuses to evoke even a glimmer of the glory that was Rome, despite all the eloquence of the guide or the detailed information of the guidebook.

This entry will not try to do more than point out some highlights of the Roman Forum, in the hope of conveying something of its importance and onetime magnificence. Those who are interested in a more detailed analysis should visit the **Museo della Civiltà Romana** in the E.U.R. (see p.64) to view its fine model of ancient Rome, and for good measure perhaps also acquire a copy of *Rome Past and Present* (Vision 1962), which has transparencies that fold back of top of photographs of the present ruins, and transforms them immediately into their imperial splendour. This is available in bookshops, including those at the Forum entrance. (NB. Touts charge more).

The Latin word *forum* means an open air market, and hence a meeting place. For the Romans, this was most conveniently situated between the Palatine hill where they made their first settlements, and the Capitol which was ultimately their seat of government. The marshy area between the two hills was drained as early at the 6th century BC, when the **Cloaca Maxima** was built (see p.89). A market grew up in the valley, around which commercial buildings known as *basilicas* were built to form a natural town centre. This gradually drew to itself banks and stock markets, administrative buildings and tax offices, law courts and places of execution, and of course (given the religiosity of the Romans) dozens of temples. Since each generation strove to be more lavish than its predecessor, buildings were superimposed on each other for 900 years, leaving not only the modern visitor but even the archæologists at their wits' end to disentangle level from level and stone from stone. The emperors themselves, aware that the overcrowding was self-defeating, eventually extended the area, and added further forums in their own name (see below). But it is this original Roman Forum that remains haunted by the ghosts of Caesar and Augustus, Virgil and Cicero, Pliny and Horace, Nero and Hadrian, Marcus Aurelius and Constantine. Walk softly, lest you tread on their dreams.

Plan of the Forum

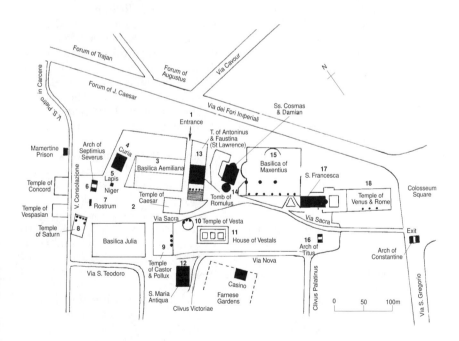

The Forum remained the civic heart of Rome until the 6th century AD. But from then on, for the thousand years in which Rome was a mere backwater, this area was no more than a convenient quarry for those who needed stone for building. The marsh returned, and became known as the **Campo Vaccino,** a grazing ground for cattle. The first archæologists had to dig through 15m of rubble to reach the buried stones. This work of cleaning and reconstructing continues.

From the entrance in the Via dei Fori Imperiali (see plan, 1), a ramp leads down to the original level. A little to the right lies the centre of the Forum (2), now an airy open area, but in classical times tightly boxed in on all four sides by imposing buildings. To the right is the platform on which stood the spacious **Basilica Æmilia** (3), one of the market's earliest commercial buildings (2nd century BC). The smaller square building ahead of it (still roofed because it was eventually turned into a church, and still serves as an exhibition centre), is the **Curia** (4), seat of the Roman Senate or House of Parliament of 300 members. Shakespeare presumed that Caesar's assassination took place here, but he was mistaken (see p.41).

Immediately ahead of where we stand is a low shelter protecting the **Lapis Niger** (5) or Black Stone, a block of marble thought to mark the tomb of Rome's legendary founder Romulus. The noble arch beyond this is one of the few ancient monuments that has survived the general dilapidation – the triumphal **Arch of Septimius Severus** (6), erected to celebrate the subjugation of Parthia (Iran) in the 3rd century AD, and still decorated with reliefs telling the story of the war. Severus later led a campaign against barbarians nearer home: from his base in York he fought the wild Scots to the north, and there died of gout. The monument, 23m high, is of course the inspiration behind London's Marble Arch and the Arc de Triomphe in Paris.

Immediately to the left of the arch is the pediment of what was once the **Rostrum** (7) from which orators could address the crowds assembled in this Trafalgar Square. The platform was named after the prows (*rostra*) of enemy ships with which it was decorated.

Behind the Rostrum, built against the sheer cliff of the Capitol hill, were two temples of which almost nothing remains. But a third, standing at right angles to the left, still proudly displays eight of its surviving columns. This **Temple of Saturn** (8) dates back to the 5th century BC, and housed the State Treasury, as well as a golden milestone recording distances to the outposts of the far-flung Roman Empire. Saturn, older even than the father-god Jupiter, was venerated by the Romans as the lord of the Golden Age and is remembered, whether consciously or not, not only every Saturday, but every Christmas when gifts are exchanged in imitation of the December Roman festival of *Saturnalia*.

Returning the way we came, back to the entrance ramp, the Forum's most distinctive feature comes into view on the right, the three isolated columns known as the 'Three Sisters' (9). This is all that remains of what was probably the Forum's most imposing building, the **Temple of Castor and Pollux,** founded like the Temple of Saturn in the 5th century BC, but embellished by the emperor Augustus in the 1st century AD. Castor and Pollux, twin sons of Jupiter and brothers of Helen of Troy, were venerated as protectors of Rome, and we meet then again, with their horses, in the approach to the Capitol (see p.43) and in front of the Quirinal Palace (see p.122).

Just to the left of the ruins of this great temple are four smaller pillars on a brick base. This is all that remains of a small circular **Temple of Vesta** (10), goddess of the hearth and the family. Here a fire was kept perpetually lit (hence our word *vesta*), from which all fires in the city were rekindled at New Year. Predictably the temple had to be rebuilt over and over again as it self-combusted, but its symbolic value was so prized ('Keep the home fires burning') that it continued to thrive for years even after the Roman religion had given way to Christianity. The sacred fire, which was regarded as a gift from the gods, was tended by a religious order of six tonsured priestesses, the Romans having none of our later scruples about ordaining women. Their convent is adjoining (11), with pediments only of a once sumptuous three-storeyed building containing fifty rooms. The cloistered courtyard still remains, surrounded by statues of past Mothers Superior. All Vestals took a vow of virginity for thirty years, under pain of a gruesome death – burial alive.

Beyond this Vestal complex, hard up against the steep slopes of the Palatine hill, is the 6th century church of **St Mary Antiqua** (12), one of the oldest Christian buildings in Rome. Much dilapidated and frequently restored, it is now more often than not closed to visitors. Which is a pity, since its walls are still bright with the forerunners of all Christian frescoes, paintings of oriental saints from the 6th to the 8th century, and a superb crucified Christ robed in royal blue, flanked by Mary and John.

Jacopone da Todi:
At the cross her station keeping,
stood the mournful mother weeping,
close to Jesus to the last.

Christ above in torment hangs,
she beneath beholds the pangs
of her dying glorious son.

By the cross with thee to stay,
there with thee to weep and pray,
is all I ask of thee to give.
    (14th century, trsl. E. Caswall)

Back once more to the entrance ramp, we face a broad flight of steps leading up to the ten remaining columns of the **Temple of Antoninus**, a 2nd century AD emperor who, with his wife Faustina, became god and goddess when they died (13). The monument is in a better state of preservation than many because it became the Christian church of **St Lawrence in Miranda,** though this is now no longer used.

Turning to the right, the **Via Sacra** leads from here to the far end of the Forum. Paved with blocks of black basalt, it was the Forum's main thoroughfare, and the route along which triumphal processions would make their way to the Capitol. A circular building on the left is known as the **Tomb of Romulus** (14), son of the 4th century emperor Maxentius. Unique in still possessing its original bronze doors, it owes its preservation to the fact that it was included in the church of **Sts Cosmas and Damian,** which is entered from outside the Forum (see p.59). It adjoins the imposing ruins of the same emperor's **Basilica of Maxentius** (15), the last of these aisled commercial buildings to be erected in the Forum. Maxentius was co-regent with Constantine, and it was the latter who actually completed the building after the power struggle which left him in sole charge: hence the colossal statue he enthroned here, 12m high, of which the pieces are still to be seen in the Conservatori Museum (see p.43). The superb arched vaults, with their span of 23m, continue to impress even in their ruin, and were the inspiration of the 16th century architects who designed St Peter's basilica.

At the top of the rise stands the Forum's last monument, and perhaps its finest, the **Arch of Titus** (16). More modest than the later arches of Septimius Severus and Constantine, it yet outshines them in elegance. Yet it celebrates a horrific event, the brutal suppression of the Jewish bid for independence in the 1st century AD, and the total destruction of Jerusalem in the year 70. Reliefs inside the arch show Titus proudly displaying the sacred Jewish emblems (branched candlestick, trumpets, table) he had looted from the Temple. A more recent Hebrew graffito stubbornly proclaims, 'The People of Israel Live Forever', though this may have been cleaned off in the restoration currently under way.

St Luke, writing about 85AD, re-tells Jesus' prediction of the fall of Jerusalem:
As some spoke of the Temple, how it was adorned with noble stones and offerings, Jesus said, 'As for these things which you see, the days will come when there shall not be left here one stone upon another that will not be thrown down'. And they asked him, 'Teacher, when will this be, and what will be the sign when this is about to take place?' And he said... 'When you see Jerusalem surrounded by armies, then know that its desolation has come near... Great distress shall be upon the earth and wrath upon this people; and they will fall by the edge of the sword, and be led captive among all nations; and Jerusalem will be trodden down by the Gentiles... Where the body is, there the (Roman) Eagles will be gathered together'.

(Luke 24: 5-24, 17: 37)

Looking down from the arch, we overlook the 10th century church of **St Mary Nuova** – (in contrast to the **Antiqua** above) – later dedicated to the Roman saint **Francesca** (17), patroness of motorcars, which line up in their hundreds around the Colosseum for a solemn blessing every 9th March. The church (entered from outside the Forum) is famous for its society weddings. To its right, an oblong mound lined with columns marks the emperor Hadrian's **Temple of Venus and Rome** (121AD) (18), of which only the stumps of pillars remain. Here one may either leave the Forum into the Colosseum square, or turn right to walk up the gentle slope of the Palatine hill (see p.102).

H.V. Morton:
People would lean [on the Forum boundary wall] all day long, peering down into the ruins as if they expected something to happen; but nothing ever does, except perhaps a cat stalking a mouse through what was once the centre of the world.

(A Traveller in Rome, p.85)

The intensive building and rebuilding on the restricted site of the Roman Forum persuaded the earliest emperors that if they were going to compete with the ancients and display buildings of their own, they would have to extend the area northwards (see plan on p.67). **Julius Caesar's** extension occupies a sunken strip between the Forum and Mussolini's Via dei Fori Imperiali, while the **Forums of Nerva and Vespasian** remain buried beneath the road. The **Forum of Augustus** survives on the far side of the road, but has little to show. To the left of it, there is however a good deal to see in the **Forum of Trajan**, the last and largest extension built in the early 2nd century AD, when the Roman Empire reached its furthest extent. The bold semi-circular market building, three storeys high, built into the hillside, remains most impressive, as does the triumphal **Trajan's Column**, erected to celebrate the subjugation of Dacia (Romania) in 106AD, the story of which is told in a spiral frieze 200m long. The column is 38m high, and an inscription claims that this was the height of the hill which Trajan excavated in order to create this forum. His golden statue once stood on top, but has long since been recycled and replaced by a bronze of St Peter. A spiral staircase inside gives access to the top, newly resplendent since its restoration in 1992.

FOUNTAIN

see under name.

FRANCESCA, Church of St.

see above.

FRASCATI

see p.142.

GARIBALDI

see p.79.

GENZANO

see p.143.

GEORGE, Church of St.

Behind S. Maria in Cosmedin. Map G3.

Historically not very important, this is nonetheless a delightful backstreet church, not very different from its neighbour **S. Maria in Cosmedin** (see p.89), and like it, dependent on the Greek Christians who once lived here, for whom St George was a hero – he only became patron of England when the crusaders brought his story to England.

Basically a 7th century basilica, with a fine baldacchino over the altar where the head of St George is reputed to be buried, it was 'renovated' over the years, but restored to its original form in 1926. When John Henry Newman was made cardinal, this was allotted to him as his titular church.

Outside, a 3rd century arch has been incorporated into the church. It is a tribute to the emperor Septimius Severus from the merchants of the cattle market which once thrived near this wharf on the river. In fact Romulus and Remus are reputed to have been washed up on this spot, before they were suckled and raised by a wolf from the Palatine above.

A second, larger and freestanding arch in the square is dedicated to the god Janus, and was erected in the 4th century to give shelter to the tradesmen in this market.

J.H. Newman:
Lead, kindly Light, amid the encircling gloom,
The night is dark, and I am far from home,
Lead thou me on.
Keep thou my feet; I do not ask to see
The distant scene; one step enough for me.

GESÙ, Church of the

On the Corso Vittorio Emmanuele, near the Monument. Map F3.

The Gesù is the principal church of the Jesuit Order in Rome, and perhaps its richest and most ornate, an epitome of the baroque style. Designed on powerful but fairly simple lines by Vignola in the 16th century, the apse, ceiling and dome were enthusiastically decorated in the following century by Baciccio, and the gorgeous marble was added a hundred years later. The body of St Ignatius, founder of the Jesuits, is buried under the elaborate altar in the left transept, guarded by Pozzo's stunning lapis lazuli and gilt columns, and Fontana's magnificent bronze altar rails.

Those brought up in the puritan tradition of the north may be surprised, perhaps even shocked, by such Mediterranean flamboyance. They will understand it better if they realise it was a Roman Catholic response to the schism which tore the western Church in two at the Reformation. Hence the lively fresco of 'heretics' being hurled out of heaven onto the heads of worshippers below. In more ecumenical days, both Protestants and Catholics may prefer to join hands to honour the name of Jesus.

Philippians 2: 5-11:
Like Adam, he was the image of God,
but unlike Adam did not presume
that being like God meant to domineer:
he knew it meant to renounce all claims,
except the claim to be servant of all.

So he lived the life of a human being,
and accepted the human fate, which is death,
even the shameful death of a slave.

That is why God has raised him up,
and given him a title beyond compare:
every creature, living and dead,
will kneel to him, and give glory to God,
and echo the cry, 'Jesus is Lord'.
(*trsl. H.J. Richards*)

Caroline M Noel:
At the name of Jesus every knee shall bow,
Every tongue confess him King of Glory now.

St Bernard:
Jesu, the very thought of thee with sweetness fills my breast,
But sweeter far thy face to see, and in thy presence rest.
(*trsl. E. Caswall*)

GHETTO

Map F3.

There was a thriving Jewish community in Rome long before the Christian era. In fact, it was among the Jews of Rome that the first Christian missionaries arriving from Palestine preached the good news of Jesus Christ. They had first settled with other foreigners in the suburb of Trastevere, and it was not until the 16th century AD that they crossed the river to establish a Jewish quarter in one of the oldest parts of Rome, along the embankment by the Tiber Island. Here they have stayed ever since, engaged mainly in the drapery trade, in the shadow of the square cupola that now crowns their synagogue (1874).

Relations between these Jews and the powerful Church that eventually dominated Rome have not always been happy. Though there were popes who defended Jewish interests (indeed they had to, since the Jews were their bankers), others imposed the most inhuman restrictions on them, enclosing them under curfew in a walled ghetto, forbidding them to own land or sell anything except clothing and discarded scrap, and demanding weekly attendance at a sermon preached at them in a church which still exists opposite the bridge to the Island (**S. Maria della Pietà**). Its façade depicts the crucified Christ and a text from the Bible in Hebrew and Latin:

I spread out my hands all the day
to a rebellious people
who follow their own devices,
a people who provoke me continually.
(*Isaiah 65: 2-3*)

This shameful programme of systematic Jew-baiting only came to an end when papal power declined in 1870. Even so there was no official protest when Mussolini collaborated with Hitler by sending

2,000 of Rome's Jews to the Auschwitz concentration camp in 1943, or, in the following year when almost a quarter of the 335 German reprisal killings were Jews (see p.61). The roots of Christian anti-semitism go deep.

Pope John XXIII (Giuseppe Roncalli) made some amends for this sad history, when in 1960 he welcomed a delegation of Jews by embracing them and saying, 'I am Joseph, your brother'. He then convoked the Vatican Council which condemned all anti-semitism, especially among the followers of Jesus the Jew. Pope John Paul II visited the synagogue in 1986 to acknowledge Christian guilt, and call for repentance.

> *Karl Barth*: There is at present much dialogue between Catholics and Protestants. But there is really only one important ecumenical question, and it is the deepest – our relationship with Israel. (1966)

GIANICOLO (Janiculum)
see p.78.

GIOVANNI
see John p.81.

GOLDEN HOUSE (Domus Aurea)

Map F4.

During the last years of his life, the psychopath emperor Nero launched a project which he hoped would make Rome thenceforth known as *Neropolis* (Nerotown). The Great Fire of 64AD (while he fiddled? he himself blamed the Christians) had razed the eastern part of the city to the ground. He proposed making this area private property, and began building on it a palace and grounds stretching from the Forum, across the dip in which the Colosseum now stands, and up the Esquiline hill to the edges of the present Lateran. The lavish project went ahead for five years. On the slopes of the hill stood the palace, plated with pure gold ('The Golden House'), with reception rooms decorated with mother of pearl, mosaic staircases down which water cascaded, bathrooms with seawater piped 26km from the Mediterranean, and a dining room whose revolving ceiling showered guests with flower petals and perfume. The corridors were lined with thousands of priceless Greek and Roman statues (the famous Laocoon group, now in the Vatican Museum p.134, was recovered from here). Outside, a colossal 30m golden statue of Nero stood sentry (see p.58). Beyond the palace, in an area of over 2.5km^2, vaster even than the present Vatican City, there were gardens, farms, woods, a zoo, and an artificial lake. When he finally took possession of this extravagant piece of self-indulgence, Nero said, 'Good, now at last I can begin to live like a human being'.

His successors Vespasian and Titus restored the whole area to the public domain, and Trajan buried the palace beneath his new baths, of which the ruins remain on the hills in the public Parco di Traiano. Access to Nero's underground folly is possible from time to time (admission charge, except for under 18's and over 60's), but the work of excavation still continues.

GREGORIAN UNIVERSITY

Piazza della Pilotta. Map E3.

The Jesuit college founded in Reformation times for the training of Catholic clergy (see p.63) was eventually named the 'Gregorian' after the pope (Gregory XIII) who enlarged it into a degree-granting university in 1583. In 1930, under Pius XI, it moved into its new premises in the Piazza della Pilotta, where it is affiliated to the adjoining Biblical Institute (1909). Students come in their thousands from all over the world, and study four or five years for a degree in theology, and then a further two years for another more specialised degree.

The Gregorian remains the largest of Rome's clerical institutes, but some religious orders also offer university degrees at the Angelicum (Dominicans), the Anselmianum (Benedictines), the Antonianum (Franciscans) and the Alfonsianum (Redemptorists).

GREGORY THE GREAT, Church of St.

Via di S. Gregorio. Map G3.

Everyone knows the story of pope Gregory asking a Roman slave-dealer about the handsome fair-haired Saxon children being offered for sale in the Forum. 'They are Angles', he was told. 'No', replied Gregory, 'they are angels'.

Whether the story is factual or not, it was certainly Gregory who in 596AD sent out a group of Benedictine monks, headed by Augustine from a Roman monastery, to take the good news of Jesus Christ to the inhospitable islands in the North Sea. Canterbury has firm roots in Rome.

The monastery still exists near the Forum, about half a km down the Via di S. Gregorio, and up a noble flight of steps on the left. The present church is a 17th century modernisation, but contains in the far chapel on the right a slab of stone on which St Gregory is said to have slept, and in the garden a chapel on the left, with a low table at which he fed twelve beggars every day, and occasionally (when an angel joined them) thirteen. Next to it, the chapel of St Andrew has murals by Domenichino and Guido Reni, but in a poor state of repair.

The monastery and church are usually closed, and permission must be gained for entrance (Tel: 700 82 87).

Prayer for England:
O blessed Virgin Mary, Mother of God,
and our most gentle Queen and Mother,
look down in mercy upon England, thy dowry,
and upon us all who greatly hope and trust in thee.
By thee it was that Jesus, our Saviour and our hope,
was given unto the world;
and he has given thee to us that we may hope still more.
Plead for us thy children, whom thou didst receive and accept
at the foot of the Cross, O sorrowful Mother!
Intercede for our separated brethren,
that with us in the one true fold
they may be united to the chief Shepherd,
the Vicar of thy Son.
Pray for us all, dear Mother,
that by faith fruitful in good works
we may all deserve to see and praise God,
together with thee, in our heavenly home.
Amen.

GROTTAFERRATA
see p.142.

HADRIAN'S VILLA (Villa Adriana)
see p.145.

HOLY STAIRS (Scala Santa)
see p.83.

IGNATIUS, Church of St.

> Piazza di S. Ignazio, west off the Via del Corso.
> Map E3.

Lavishly baroque like its sister church, The Gesù (see p.73), this church was built in the mid 17th century in honour of the founder of the Jesuit order, who was declared a saint only 37 years after his death. The interior decor is the work of a Jesuit priest, Andrea del Pozzo, who knew all there was to be known about perspective. Since the plans for a central dome had to be abandoned, he decided to give the impression of one from the inside by painting it onto the flat ceiling. Find the marble disc in the floor to view it (if necessary by switching the illumination on with a coin), and see how brilliantly he succeeded.

Robert Bellarmine is buried in the third chapel on the right, and Aloysius Gonzaga and John Berchmans in the right transept. All these three Jesuits have been canonised.

Backing onto the church is the **Collegio Romano**, which occupies the whole block up to the spacious Piazza del Collegio Romano. It was one of the first colleges to answer the Council of Trent's call for new institutions to train the post-Reformation clergy. Founded by the Jesuits in 1551, many of the English martyrs did their studies here before returning to England. The Gregorian University (see p.76) took its place when the college was commandeered in 1870, and it is now mainly a museum and a library, enjoying (like the British Museum) the right to a free copy of all works published in the country.

IMMACULATE CONCEPTION
see p.36.

JANICULUM (Gianicolo)

To the west of the Tiber, beyond Trastevere, the Janiculum hill is not numbered among the traditional 'Seven' (see p.125), but since the 3rd century AD has been included in the city walls. On top there is a large public park, providing a marvellous panorama of Rome and the mountains beyond, best in the afternoon and evening light. The tree-lined walk through the park is decorated with the busts of patriots, some now noseless, and leads to a square dominated by the bronze equestrian **Monument to Garibaldi** (1), the 19th century leader of the struggle for Italian unity: in fact it was on these heights that the final decisive battle was fought.

A little further on there is a smaller bronze monument to Garibaldi's Brazilian guerrilla wife Anita (2). She is riding a fiery steed, one hand holding a gun, and the other cradling her baby. He had wooed her, he tells us, by simply picking her out of a group of girls and saying, 'Young lady, you'll be mine'. Further along still, there is a small lighthouse (*faro*) (3) which at night flashes out the Italian national colours, green, white and red, a gift in 1911 from South American Italians, in gratitude for Garibaldi's efforts to achieve the independence of Argentina.

Visitors should be warned that every midday a cannon is fired from this hill to tell everyone in Rome what time it is.

The angel of the Lord declared unto Mary,
And she conceived by the Holy Ghost.
> Hail Mary, full of grace, the Lord is with thee,
> blessed art thou among women,
> and blessed is the fruit of thy womb, Jesus.
> Holy Mary, Mother of God, pray for us sinners,
> now and at the hour of our death. Amen.

Behold the handmaid of the Lord,
Be it done unto me according to thy word. Hail Mary, etc.

And the Word was made flesh,
And dwelt amongst us. Hail Mary, etc.

Pray for us, O holy Mother of God,
That we may be made worthy of the promises of Christ.

Let us pray.
Pour forth, we beseech thee, O Lord,
thy grace into our hearts;
that we, to whom the Incarnation of Christ thy Son
was made known by the message of an angel,
may, by his Passion and Cross,
be brought to the glory of his Resurrection.
Through the same Christ our Lord. Amen.

Not far from the Monument are a number of other worthwhile sights on this hill, each with a view quite as magnificent, especially at sunset. Further downhill from the lighthouse is the delightful little church built in honour of the 4th century hermit **St Onofrio** (Humphrey?) (4), friend of the more famous Paphnutius, who campaigned for the ordination of married men. In the 15th century it became a monastery of the monks of St Jerome, and is now looked after by the American Friars of the Atonement. Its simple cloister has some wonderfully naïve frescoes of the life of St Onofrio, and the life of St Jerome is depicted by Domenichino in the church porch. Inside, the church glows with more frescoes in the apse, possibly by Pinturicchio. The Italian poet Tasso, a contemporary of Shakespeare, ended his days in this monastery. The blasted oak under which he used to like to sit and think is a little further up the hill (5).

> *Tasso*:
> Love, while youth knows its prime.
> For mortal life can make no truce with time.
> Love: for the sun goes down to rise as bright;
> To us his transient light
> Is veiled, and sleep comes on with everlasting night.
> *Aminta*
> *(trsl. Thomas Love Peacock)*

On the opposite side of the Monument, going south down the winding Via Garibaldi, one comes to the church of **St Peter in Montorio** (6), built in the 15th century by Ferdinand and Isabella of Spain because of the early legend that this is where St Peter was martyred. It is a highly unlikely spot, but contains some fine 16th century paintings. Raphael's *Transfiguration* (see p.134) once hung here, until it was looted by Napoleon and eventually returned to the Vatican. To the right of the church is the tiny Renaissance temple (*tempietto*: it holds only ten people) set up here by Bramante in 1502 as an exercise in proportion and symmetry. Those interested in architecture will find it a delight of grace and harmony, worth coming a long way to see.

JOHN AND PAUL, Church of Sts.
(Santi Giovanni e Paulo)

Clivo di Scauro, near the Colosseum. Map G4.

Recent excavations under this church have revealed that, from the 2nd century onwards, Christians met and worshipped on this spot, where a hundred years earlier Nero had walked in the gardens of his Golden House. On a later level has been found the tomb of martyrs, and frescoes of the 5th century indicating that their memory was venerated here. This adds substance to the old tradition that this was the house of two of Constantine's court officials, martyred by his apostate successor Julian in the 4th century.

The present buildings have remains of a more elaborate 12th century church (whose porch was built by the only English pope, Nicholas Breakspear who became Adrian IV), and a bell tower and cosmati pavement from the 13th century, when the frescoes of a chapel in the left aisle were also painted. The rest of the church is from the 18th century, when the remains of John and Paul were laid in a porphyry tomb.

The adjoining monastery was also built in the 18th century as the headquarters of St Paul of the Cross, founder of the Passionist Order, now buried in a domed chapel off the right aisle of the church. In the 19th century the monastery was the home of the Passionist priests Bl. Dominic Barberi (who received Newman into the Catholic Church), and of Ignatius Spencer, great-uncle of Winston Churchill, and a more distant relative of Lady Diana Spencer, HRH Princess of Wales.

JOHN LATERAN, Basilica of St.
(S. Giovanni in Laterano)

Metro A, S. Giovanni. Map G4.

Those who still read Latin may be surprised that this church is described, on its façade, as 'Mother and Head of all Churches in Rome and in the World': they thought such words could apply only to St Peter's. The fact is that it was on this hill, not on the Vatican, that the first public Christian church was built by Constantine in the 4th century, on property he had confiscated from the patrician Laterani family (hence the name). The palace alongside was the official residence of all the popes from the 4th century to the 14th, and even after they moved to the Vatican, the Lateran remained the site of the papal *cathedra* or throne. The earliest solemn Councils of the Church to be convened in the west took place here. As late as 1929, the agreement between the Italian State and the Catholic Church was known not as the Vatican Treaty, but the Lateran Treaty.

The original 4th century church was dedicated to the Saviour, though the importance attached to the adjoining baptistry has allowed John the Baptist to take over the name. The present building is the end result of several remodellings, most notably by Borromini in the 17th century, who restored its ancient simple basilica form, but bestowed on it a colder atmosphere than is felt in any other of the major churches. The main entrance is in the Piazza Porta S. Giovanni, with its modern monument of St Francis of Assisi symbolically preventing the church (The Church) from collapsing. The 18th century façade is topped by fifteen colossal statues of Christ, John the Baptist, John the Evangelist, and the twelve saints acclaimed as Doctors (teachers) of the Church.

Inside, between the plastered pillars of the nave, the twelve apostles appear in baroque splendour. Ahead, the high altar is covered by a gothic canopy which is said to contain the heads of St Peter and St Paul in silver reliquaries, and the wooden table used by St Peter to celebrate the Eucharist (see p.120). Beyond, in the apse is a reconstruction of the original 4th century mosaics, showing Christ the Saviour surrounded by angels and saints, who now include Francis of Assisi and Antony of Padua. The left aisle leads to a door into the 13th century cloister, gorgeous in cosmati work (closed Sun, and daily 12.30-15.00. Admission charge).

John 4: 40-42: When the Samaritans came to Jesus, they asked him to stay with them; and he stayed there two days. And many more believed because of his word. They said to the woman, 'It is no longer because of your words that we believe, for we have heard for ourselves, and we know that this is indeed the *Saviour* of the world'.

Titus 2: 11-13: The grace of God has appeared for the salvation of all men, training us to renounce irreligion and worldly passions, and to live sober, upright, and godly lives in this world, awaiting our blessed hope, the appearing of the glory of the great God and of our *Saviour* Jesus Christ.

Aurelius Prudentius:
Of the Father's love begotten,
ere the worlds began to be,
he is Alpha and Omega,
he the source, the ending he,
of all things that are and have been
and that future years shall see:
evermore and evermore.
(trsl. J.M. Neale)

At the top of the right aisle is a side exit to the spacious **Piazza S. Giovanni**, which is dominated by the largest Egyptian obelisk in existence (see p.101). It measures 32m and weighs 500,000kg, and was commissioned by the same pharaoh as had London's Cleopatra's Needle cut for him. Any reader of hieroglyphs will spot the misprint on the west side of the obelisk; and any Latin scholar will point out the historical error inscribed into the base, which ascribes Constantine's baptism to this spot, whereas in fact it only took place on his deathbed abroad. Constantine was the sort of man who did not want his sins remitted until he'd got them all committed.

Off the piazza is the beautiful octagonal **Baptistry**, a 4th century dome supported on eight porphyry columns over a noble basalt bath, surrounded by four small chapels. The chapel on the right, dedicated to John the Baptist, has bronze doors 'rescued' from the Baths of Caracalla (see p.36) which sing like an organ when moved in their sockets. (Ask the sacristan, or hope that someone else has paid him to do so while you are there). H.V. Morton compares the sound to the agonised cry of a pagan imprisoned by Christians. (No admission charge, but closed 12.00-15.30).

Romans 6: 3-4: Do you not know that all of us who have been baptised into Christ Jesus were baptised into his death? We were buried therefore with him by baptism into death, so that as Christ was raised from the dead by the glory of the Father, we too might walk in newness of life.

Titus 3: 4-7: When the goodness and loving kindness of God our Saviour appeared, he saved us, not because of deeds done by us in righteousness, but in virtue of his own mercy, by the washing of regeneration and renewal in the Holy Spirit, which he poured out upon us richly through Jesus Christ our Saviour, so that we might be justified by his grace and become heirs in hope of eternal life.

The palace at the other end of the piazza is the **Lateran Palace** as rebuilt in the 16th century. It houses the administration for the diocese of Rome. The older palace lay further to the right, and incorporated the **Scala Santa** or Holy Stairs which are now in a separate building across the road. Made of marble, the 28 steps are now covered in wood, and at all times of the year, but especially in Holy Week, pilgrims will be found ascending the steps on their knees. Entrance is free daily, 8.00-12.00 and 15.30-19.00.

Popular tradition has it that this was the actual *Scala Pilati* (Pilate's Stairway) which Jesus would have gone up during his trial in the Roman Praetorium in Jerusalem. Some scholars have suggested that the steps are no more than the *Scala Palatii* (Palace Stairway) to gain access to the chapel at the top. Whichever, the painful ascent provides a worthwhile sharing in the suffering of Jesus and of all his disciples through the ages (Martin Luther made the ascent but abandoned it halfway), not least of those suffering in the Third World. The brilliant 13th century cosmati work (geometrical marble fragments) in the chapel is unfortunately only visible through a grate. Two side stairways are provided for the descent. Turn left as you come out, to see the mosaic on the wall outside. It dates from 800AD, and once decorated the papal dining room to celebrate the coronation of Charlemagne as Holy Roman Emperor.

John 18: 28-19: 5: They led Jesus from the house of Caiaphas to the Praetorium... Pilate went out to them and said, 'What accusation do you bring against this man?' They answered him, 'If this man were not an evil-doer, we would not have handed him over' ... Pilate entered the Praetorium again and called Jesus, and said to him, 'Are you the King of the Jews?' ... Jesus answered, 'My kingship is not of this world.' ... Pilate said to him, 'So you are a king?' Jesus answered, ' "King" is your word. What I was born for, and what I have come into the world for, is to bear witness to the truth.' Pilate said to him, 'What is truth?'

Then Pilate took Jesus and scourged him. And the soldiers plaited a crown of thorns, and put it on his head, and arrayed him in a purple robe, like a Roman Emperor. They came up to him, saying, 'Hail, King of the Jews!' and struck him with their hands. Pilate went out again and said to them, 'See, I am bringing him out to you, that you may know that I find no crime in him'. So Jesus came out, wearing the crown of thorns and the purple robe. Pilate said to them, 'Behold the man!'

Visitors to the Lateran may be interested to know that a daily clothes market is held just outside the city walls at this point.

KEATS MEMORIAL
see p.118.

KEYHOLE VIEW
see p.124.

KNIGHTS OF MALTA, Priory of the
see p.124.

LATERAN, Basilica of St John.
see p.81.

LAWRENCE IN DAMASO
see p.42.

LAWRENCE OUTSIDE THE WALLS, Church of St. (S. Lorenzo fuori le mura)

Via Tiburtina, a kilometre beyond the north east wall. Map E5.

The legend of St Lawrence tells us that, as one of the pope's seven deacons, he was responsible for Rome's poor, a sort of one-man SVP. Captured in a 3rd century persecution, he was ordered to reveal where the Church's treasures were. He did so: he led in a procession of his beggars. He was roasted alive on a gridiron, and had the wit (like Thomas More's 'Mind my beard: it's no traitor') to make a final wisecrack: 'This side's done; turn me over'.

Constantine built a church over the catacomb where Lawrence was buried – hence the inclusion of this venerable church among the traditional 'Seven' (see p.174). In the 6th century this became a basilica, to which was added, head on, a much larger one in the 13th century. The exact relation of these two churches remained a mystery, which was paradoxically solved when allied planes dropped a bomb on the place in 1943 (it is close to Rome's railway marshalling yards) and forced much restoration work.

The main entrance (recently cleaned in 1993) leads into the later church, whose fine proportions are enhanced by the inlaid cosmati pavement and the 13th century frescoes of the deacons Lawrence and Stephen. The raised choir has two fine pulpits (*ambones*) in the same cosmati style, the righthand one being acclaimed as the finest in Rome. The altar stands over the crypt where St Lawrence is buried – accompanied, it is said, by St Stephen, whose remains were brought here via Constantinople. There are stairs down into this crypt.

Upstairs again, it is worth looking back down the church to see the fine 6th century mosaics on the back of the arch spanning the church at this point: Christ in glory is attended by Sts Peter and Paul, Lawrence and Stephen and others, the whole framed between Bethlehem and Jerusalem. Beyond the high altar the church continues, but now as the first floor of the older 6th century church, whose pillars poke through the floor to support the extended ceiling. At the end, a beautiful 13th century decorative throne for the bishop.

Entrance to the older church is by steps in the side aisles leading to the back of the tombs in the crypt just visited. Another tomb at the far end of this older church is that of pope Pius IX (Pio Nono) who died in 1878. He was offered a spot in Mary Major's, but chose to be buried here among the poor. So did de Gasperi, the post-war statesman who spent his life working for a united Europe. Back upstairs, the right aisle will take you to the sacristy, which has a shop served by the Franciscans who are in charge of the church. Beyond the sacristy is a charming 11th century cloister, displaying the remains of the 1943 bomb.

Adjacent to the church is the Campo Verano, Rome's main cemetery, where the remains of the dead are gathered after a number of years and stored in monuments above ground.

LENT STATIONS
see p.168.

LORENZO, see Lawrence.

LOUIS, Church of St. (S. Luigi)

Piazza S. Luigi near the Pantheon. Map E2.

Louis IX, the 13th century king of France who went to Jerusalem to bring back the Crown of Thorns still venerated in the Sainte Chapelle in Paris, and who died in the east on his way to another Crusade, was acclaimed as a saint soon after his death. His cult spread quickly, and when French pilgrims wanted a church of their own in Rome, they named it after him. The present noble renaissance building was put up by Fontana in the 1580's, a time when St Peter's was not yet completed. In the 17th century it was enriched by two outstanding works of art – Domenichino's gentle fresco of St Cecilia in the second chapel on the right, and further up the left aisle Caravaggio's chapel of St Matthew, with three scenes from his life, as disciple, as evangelist, and as martyr. Caravaggio died at the age of 37, after a lifetime of police records. This did not endear him to the clergy, who found his dramatic realism far too disrespectful to the holy apostle. But these three canvases are now recognised as perhaps the finest he ever painted. (There are more Caravaggios in St Augustine's nearby, see p.34).

Matthew 9: 9-13:
As Jesus passed on from there, he saw a man called Matthew sitting at the tax office; and he said to him, 'Follow me.' And he rose and followed him. And as he sat at table in the house, behold, many tax collectors and sinners came and sat down with Jesus and his disciples. And when the Pharisees saw this, they said to his disciples, 'Why does your teacher eat with tax collectors and sinners?' But when he heard it, he said, 'Those who are well have no need of a physician, but those who are sick. Go and learn what this means, "I desire mercy, and not sacrifice." For I came not to call the righteous, but sinners.'

LUIGI
see above.

MAMERTINE PRISON (Carcer Mamertinus)

Map F3. Admission by donation, 9.00-12.30, and 14.30-19.30.

At the end of a flight of steps at the southern end of Capitol Hill (see plan p.42), and divided from the Forum by a road, are the two gloomy cells in which the ancient Romans imprisoned their conquered enemies. Plaques commemorate the Goth leader Jugurtha, and the Gaul Vercingetorix. The lower cell has an altar where Mass may be celebrated. It is dedicated to St Peter, whom legend reports as creating a miraculous spring of water to baptise his jailers. The story is presumably dependent on that of Paul's imprisonment in Asia Minor in Acts 16. The same book tells us that Paul was also imprisoned in Rome, but in much milder circumstances.

Acts 28: 16, 30-31:
When we came into Rome, Paul was allowed to stay by himself, with the soldier that guarded him... And he lived there two whole years at his own expense, and welcomed all who came to him, preaching the kingdom of God and teaching about the Lord Jesus Christ quite openly and unhindered.

MARCELLUS, Theatre of.

Between the Capitol and the Tiber.
See plan p.104.

Nearly a century before the double theatre (*amphi-theatrum*) of the Colosseum was built, Julius Caesar built a single one nearer the river. It was completed by Augustus in 13BC, and named after his hoped-for successor Marcellus. It could entertain 20,000 spectators who came to watch plays, operas, pantomimes and other spectacles. In classical times it was surrounded by a vast vegetable market (*forum olitorium*) and cattle market (*forum boarium*) stretching down to the river. In the Middle Ages, long abandoned, it became a fortress, and later (in its upper storey) a Renaissance palace. It remains today a complex of apartments, though archæologists continue (since 1989) to excavate beneath.

In front, three Corinthian columns remain of a temple to Apollo dating back to the 5th century BC, now only an elegant ruin.

MARFORIO
see p.43.

MARINO
see p.142.

MARK, St
see p.99.

MARY (ANGELS)
see p.37.

MARY (ANTIQUA)
see p.69.

MARY (ARACOELI), Church of St.

Above the Capitol. See plan p.104.

Some wonderful stories and legends are attached to this church, perched on a promontory of its own high above the Capitol hill. From the 6th century BC the Romans trudged up this hill to a temple built in honour of Jupiter's consort Juno, the Queen of Heaven. She was honoured for warning her people of any danger, as when her sacred geese raised the alarm during the attempt of the

Gauls to take this citadel secretly by night. So her title became *Juno Moneta* ('Alarm Bell'). Since the Roman Mint was adjoining, the coins produced were also called *moneta*, giving the western world the words *moneda*, *münze*, *monnaie*, and *money*.

Later, a Sybil is said to have revealed to the emperor Augustus, in this temple of Juno, that a virgin would bear a divine child. He therefore built here an 'Altar of Heaven' (*ara coeli*, hence the name) with the inscription 'Behold the Altar of the Firstborn of God'. This inscription has been reproduced on the arch of a chapel in the left transept of the present church, where a porphyry urn contains the remains of St Helena, mother of the emperor Constantine; and in a chapel on the right, a Pinturicchio *Madonna* is unashamedly flanked by Augustus and his Sybil, as if they were honorary Christians.

Constantine's liberation of the long-persecuted Christian community led to the building of many churches, but it was not till the 6th century AD that a Christian church replaced the pagan temple on this rather inaccessible hill. The Franciscans enlarged it into the present church in the 13th century, and a hundred year later added the 124 steps to help visitors. Present day pilgrims, with less sturdy legs, may find it more convenient to approach it by a much shorter flight of stairs from the Capitol piazza. These lead into the church by a side door.

The original simple basilica plan still predominates, with aisles formed by mismatching columns taken from an assortment of classical buildings. The floor is studded with gravestones ancient and modern. The coffered ceiling was totally refurbished in 1571 to celebrate the crucial defeat of the Turks at Lepanto.

Time should be taken to see the chapels mentioned above, but above all the Sacristy, where the Holy Child (*Santo Bambino*) is displayed in a glass case. Carved in the 17th century from Gethsemane olive wood and clothed in a heavily bejewelled gown, it used to be taken regularly to any severely sick person in Rome who asked, but really comes into its own over the Christmas season, when it is brought out into the nave for Rome's children to recite their pieces before it. On Christmas Eve, the front stairway is thronged with shepherds playing their pipes, while the *Bambino* is brought out to call down God's blessing on the city.

It was in this church, with its bird's eye view of the ruined Forum (see p.42) that Gibbon's classic *The Decline and Fall of the Roman Empire* was born. He was 27. He was 50 before he finished it.

Edward Gibbon:
It was at Rome, on the 15th of October, 1764, as I sat musing amidst the ruins of the Capitol, while the barefooted friars were singing

vespers in the Temple of Jupiter (*correction*, Juno), that the idea of writing the decline and fall of the city first started to my mind.

Regina cœli, lætare, alleluia
Quia quem meruisti portare, alleluia
Resurrexit, sicut dixit, alleluia
Ora pro nobis Deum, alleluia.

Queen of heaven, shout for joy, alleluia
The one you bore and raised as a boy, alleluia
Has been raised from the dead, just as he said, alleluia
Pray with us to God our Father, alleluia.

MARY (COSMEDIN), Church of St.

Left bank near the Island. Map G3.

One of Rome's oldest churches, built in the 6th century for a colony of Greek Christians. In its present form it is a 19th century restoration, but the restorers have successfully preserved for us the kind of basilica church in which our mediæval brothers and sisters worshipped. The 12th century marble pavement in the church, and the bell-tower outside, stand out as perhaps the finest in Rome.

The church is particularly well known for the monstrous marble **Bocca della Verità** (Mouth of Truth) standing in the porch. It is an ancient Roman drain cover, but became a popular lie detector. Those suspected of lying, particularly about adultery, had to swear with their hand inside the gaping mouth which (it was threatened) would bite off any liar's fingers. Most people wisely spoke the truth.

Talking of drains, anyone taking a few steps onto the nearby bridge (Ponte Palatino) and looking left downstream, can see the three arches through which the ancient Roman main sewer (**Cloaca Maxima**) was emptied into the river.

Between the church and the river stand two charming little temples, one circular and one rectangular, remarkably unscathed survivors from classical times. They date from about 100BC, and stood in the market which was attached to the river wharf where merchandise from overseas was unloaded. It is anyone's guess to whom these temples were dedicated, since archæologists disagree. But one can be grateful that the human race's perennial search for God has, amidst all its horrors, also produced beauty like this.

Ave Regina coelorum
Ave Domina angelorum
Salve radix, salve porta
Ex qua mundo lux est orta
Gaude Virgo gloriosa

Super omnes speciosa
Vale o valde decora
Et pro nobis Christum exora.

Hail, O Queen of heaven enthroned!
Hail, by angels mistress owned,
Root of Jesse! Gate of morn!
Whence the world's true light was born.
Glorious Virgin, joy to thee,
Loveliest whom in heaven they see.
Fairest thou where all are fair!
Plead with Christ our sins to spare.

MARY, St. (IMMACULATE)

see p.36.

MARY (MAJOR), Basilica of St. (Maria Maggiore)

Near Termini Station (Metro A and B, Termini).
Map F4.

Of the eighty Roman churches dedicated to Our Lady, this is the greatest (*maggiore*). Its situation is based on the legend that snow fell on this Esquiline hill one August in the 4th century, and that the dreaming pope Liberius was told by Our Lady to build a church on the spot (according to a refinement of the story, the snowfall gave exact specifications of the groundplan). A church was accordingly built, and every 5th August since, the feast of 'Our Lady of the Snows', white rose petals are showered down from the dome to recall the delightful story. Or should one only delight in stories about hard fact?

In the following century, 431AD, all the bishops of the world met at Ephesus in Asia Minor to condemn the heretic Nestorius, who held that Mary was only the mother of the human Jesus, not of the divine Christ. Jesus was only one person, said the bishops, and Mary is rightly called *Theotokos*, the God-bearer. To celebrate this fundamental statement, the church was enlarged into a stately three-aisled basilica. Even though elaborate side-chapels were added later, and the whole structure eventually encased in an 18th century baroque shell, it is this gorgeous 5th century church skilfully restored, which still basically exists, and which the pilgrim still enters today.

The west end of the church (Via Cavour and Via De Pretis), with its obelisk and gracious flight of steps, might give one the impression that this is the main door. But in fact it is the back of the church, and the entrance is at the east from the Via Merulana. This too has a piazza and a classical column topped with a statue of Our Lady.

From the column, the 14th century façade mosaics can be seen behind the arched openings – if the light is right.

One enters a nave paved with fine 12th century cosmati work, flanked by matching marble columns, and roofed in by a coffered ceiling gilded with the first gold brought back in 1500 from the Americas, a gift from Ferdinand and Isabella of Spain. Between ceiling and columns, there is a whole series of 5th century mosaics, sadly not easily discernible by the naked eye. But the same mosaics, extraordinarily well preserved, continue on the triumphal arch which is more easily read. They tell the story, quite brilliantly, of the Infancy gospel, with Mary as a Byzantine princess, and the pope's own signature: 'Bishop Sixtus to the People of God'. Beyond, the extended apse continues to extol Mary, now enthroned alongside Christ, who places a crown on her head. This glorious mosaic is from the 13th century.

Under the arch, the altar is covered by an elaborate 18th century canopy. In a railed recess in front of it, steps lead down to a casket containing five pieces of wood claiming to be part of Jesus' Bethlehem crib. Alongside, appropriately enough, are the relics of the 4th century Scripture scholar Jerome, who spent years in the Bethlehem cave to produce a bible which the west would understand – the Latin Vulgate. A statue of pope Pius IX kneels to venerate the relics, which are displayed on the 25th of each month, and of course over the Christmas season.

Back in the nave are two large domed side-chapels added in the 16th century. To the right (facing the high altar) is the Blessed Sacrament chapel, built by Fontana for the obelisk enthusiast Sixtus V (hence **Sistine Chapel**). Next to it is the **Holy Relics Chapel**, containing the cranium of the English St Thomas of Canterbury, and his hairshirt. Opposite on the left, and in clear competition, is the Lady Chapel built for the Borghese pope Paul V (hence **Pauline Chapel**), rich in jasper, agate, amethyst and lapis lazuli. The altar has a venerable icon of Our Lady attributed (like many others) to the evangelist St Luke. Experts say they are the work of an 8th century icon painter called Sanlucca. It is adjoined by a chapel designed for the Sforza family by Michelangelo.

The church is cared for by Redemptorists. A rota of Dominicans are in attendance at all times to hear confessions in all languages.

Salve Regina, mater misericordiae
Vita, dulcedo, et spes nostra, salve.
Ad te clamamus, exsules filii Hevae;
Ad te suspiramus, gementes et flentes
In hac lacrimarum valle.
Eia ergo, advocata nostra
Illos tuos misericordes oculos ad nos converte.
Et Jesum, benedictum fructum ventris tui,
Nobis post hoc exsilium ostende.
O clemens, o pia, o dulcis Virgo Maria.

Hail holy Queen, mother of mercy
Hail our life, our sweetness and our hope.
To thee do we cry, poor banished children of Eve;
To thee do we send up our sighs
Mourning and weeping in this vale of tears.
Turn then, most gracious advocate
Thine eyes of mercy towards us
And after this our exile
Show unto us the blessed fruit of thy womb, Jesus.
O clement, O loving, O sweet Virgin Mary.

Jacopone da Todi:
In my morning prayer
I saw LOVE written
upon every creature:
men on their foreheads,
trees on their flowers,
houses on their walls.
CHRIST has flowered in man's flesh:
let human nature rejoice!
(*trsl: Daniel Berrigan*)

MARY (MINERVA), Church of St.

Piazza della Minerva, near the Pantheon. Map F3.

A Christian church was built here, on the ruins of a temple of Minerva (hence the name) as early as 800AD. The present building dates from the 13th century, and it has been considerably altered and added to since. Nonetheless it remains the only gothic church in Rome, and brings some relief to those who have had a surfeit of baroque. The façade has undergone a recent much-needed spring-clean.

Inside, the popularity of the church over the ages is marked by the numerous memorials set into the walls and floor, and by the abundance of works of art, the most outstanding of which is the lovely chapel in the right transept, frescoed throughout by Filippino Lippi in the 15th century in honour of Our Lady, and the Dominican saint Thomas Aquinas (a slot machine gives illumination). Under the high altar lies the body of Italy's patron saint, the Dominican Catherine of Siena who died at the age of 33, worn out by her arguments with the 14th century Avignon popes. Romans have no hesitation in going right up the altar steps to pay their respects. To the left of the altar stands Michelangelo's magnificent *Risen Christ*, protected now from kissers by bronze shoes, and from prudes by an added loincloth. Further to the left, in a corridor, is the tomb of the gentle Dominican artist Fra Angelico.

The monastery next to the church is the headquarters of the Dominican Order. Given the gentleness of Thomas Aquinas, Catherine and Fra Angelico, how did the Dominicans ever come to preside over the 'Holy' Inquisition? It was in this monastery that Galileo was tried. Aware of the number of 'heretics' who had been burnt in the **Piazza della Minerva** outside (an 'act of faith' the Inquisition called it, an *auto da fé*), he wisely decided to agree with his captors that the earth does *not* go round the sun. But he is said to have muttered as he left the court, 'It jolly well does'. Today the piazza is a more gentle place, graced by the little pyramid balanced on the back of Bernini's elephant. 'A parable of the need for wisdom to be based on a solid foundation', proclaims the inscription of pope Alexander VII, clearly as foxed by the hieroglyphs as the taxi driver who was heard to explain to his fare that it was a signpost from an Egyptian zoo.

Luke 1: 46-55: My soul magnifies the Lord,
my spirit rejoices in God, my Saviour.
He looks on his servant in her nothingness;
henceforth all ages will call me blessed.
The Almighty works marvels for me.
Holy his name!
His mercy is from age to age
on those who fear him.
He puts forth his arm in strength
and scatters the proudhearted.
he casts the mighty from their thrones
and raises the lowly.
He fills the starving with good things,
sends the rich away empty.
He protects Israel, his servant,
remembering his mercy
the mercy promised to our fathers,
for Abraham and his sons for ever.

(*Grail*)

P. De Rosa: Father, I thank you for what you have revealed of yourself
in Mary's virgin motherhood.
She was humble so you exalted her;
she was poor so you enriched her;
she was empty so you filled her;
she was your servant so you cared for her;
she had no future by reason of her virginity,
so you brought to birth in her
the world's future, Jesus Christ our Lord.

MARY (POPOLO), Church of St.

Piazza del Popolo. Metro A, Flaminio, Map D3.

'Blessed is he who comes' is the greeting with which pilgrims were once welcomed into Jerusalem (Psalm 118: 26), and indeed still are in many towns in the Holy Land. A similar greeting, 'A happy and blessed entrance', is inscribed in Latin on Bernini's inner façade of Rome's northern gate leading in from the Via Flaminia, and so known both as **Porta Flaminia** and **Porta del Popolo**. Until railways were invented, this was where all travellers to Rome arrived and left. The gate opens onto the magnificent oval **Piazza del Popolo**, designed in the last century by Valadier to provide an impressive first impression, with its fine central obelisk (see p.101), and its perfectly balanced two Bernini churches ahead, separating the three roads that lead into the heart of Rome.

The piazza is a popular rallying point for political meetings, as its name seems to suggest. In fact the name is taken from the church of St Mary del Popolo after the poplars that once grew there, reputedly over Nero's family tomb. The noisy crows that nested in them were thought to be Nero's ghost, and by popular request they were cut down.

The church dates from the 11th century, but it was re-designed by Bernini, and some of his work is to be seen inside as well. Indeed the church is a veritable treasure house of fine pieces by Pinturicchio (ceiling and first chapel on the right), Fontana, Raphael, Sansovino, del Piombo and Caravaggio (last chapel on the left). The church was at one time connected with an Augustinian monastery, in which Martin Luther stayed from 1510-1511.

Luther:
Hail holy Rome,
sanctified by the holy martyrs,
and by the blood they shed there.
(*On arriving in Rome in 1510*).

Alma Redemptoris mater
quae pervia coeli porta manes, et stella maris,
succurre cadenti surgere qui curat populo.
Tu quae genuisti, natura mirante,
tuum sanctum Genitorem.
Virgo prius, ac posterius,
Gabrielis ab ore, sumens illud Ave,
peccatorum miserere.

Loving mother of the Redeemer,
open door to heaven, and star of the sea,
come to the aid of your people,
fallen but striving to stand again.
To the astonishment of Nature,

you were mother of your holy Creator
without ceasing to be a virgin,
and heard from Gabriel that greeting 'Hail':
take pity on us sinners.

Cardinal Wiseman: Catholic England has been restored to its orbit in
the ecclesiastical firmament, from which its light had long vanished,
and begins anew its course of regularly adjusted action round the
centre of unity (Rome), the source of jurisdiction, of light and of
vigour... We govern, and shall continue to govern, the counties of
Middlesex, Hertford and Essex, as Ordinary thereof, with the islands
annexed, as administrator with ordinary jurisdiction.
(A Pastoral Letter, *Out of the Flaminian Gate*, sent to announce his return
to England after the restoration of the English Roman Catholic
hierarchy, 7th October 1850).

Queen Victoria's reply: Am I the Queen of England, or am I not?

MARY (PIETÀ)
see p.74.

MARY (TRASTEVERE), Church of St.
Piazza S. Maria in Trastevere. Map G2.

This church claims the honour of being Rome's oldest Marian
church still in use, founded in the 3rd century (even before the
Roman Empire became Christian) on a spot where legend said oil
began to flow from the earth on the first Christmas day. The present
building is the result of later developments in romanesque and
baroque times.

The 12th and 13th century contributed the bell tower, the
glorious mosaic façade of Our Lady with saints, the cosmati
pavement inside, and the quite brilliant Cavallini mosaics that fill
the apse (the *Coronation of Mary*, surrounded by scenes from her
life). The 19th century contributed the ornate canopy over the
altar. British visitors should look for a chapel to the right of the
altar, which bears their royal coat of arms, because it was restored
by the Stuart cardinal who claimed to be the legitimate Duke of
York in the 18th century. The English Benedictine cardinal
Gasquet lived in the Benedictine monastery to the left of the
church.

Outside the church, the piazza has a 17th century raised
fountain designed by Fontana, and cafés where people love to
meet, sit and talk. Crowds come on 15th August, the patronal feast
of the Assumption of Our Lady, when there are processions, floats
and fireworks.

Revelation 12: 1-5:
In the sky I saw a woman.
Her clothes were as dazzling as the sun.
She stood with the moon under her feet,
and twelve stars formed a crown for her head.
She gave birth to a baby boy,
who was going to be king of all the world.

MARY (VALLICELLA), Church of St. (Chiesa Nuova)

On the north side of the Corso Vittorio
Emmanuele, near the river. Map F2.

St Philip Neri, hero of counter-reformation Rome, where he was
known for his gentle and laid-back approach as *Pippo Buono* ('Good
Old Phil'), founded his Congregation of Oratorians in 1575. It was
so immediately successful that two years later he was able to
commission the building of this magnificent baroque structure on
top of an older church of Our Lady. It has been known ever since
as the New Church (**Chiesa Nuova**). The interior is simple and in
white, as Philip had specified, but the ceiling and dome were
eventually generously decorated by Cortona, and three fine Rubens
paintings were added to the altar in 1608. At the end of the left aisle
is the tomb of the saint, in marble and mother of pearl, and the
sacristy commemorates this giant of a man with an appropriately
gigantic statue. The mother-house of the congregation, known as
the Oratory, adjoins the church. Its fascinating curved façade is by
Borromini, 1650.

Romans 5: 5, Psalm 103: 1:
God's love has been poured into our hearts through the Holy Spirit
which has been given to us. Bless the Lord, O my soul, and all that is
within me, bless his holy name!
(*Introit to the Mass of St Philip Neri*).

MARY (VICTORY), Church of St. (S. Maria della Vittoria)

Via XX Settembre. Map E3.

The 'victory' refers to the battle near Prague that ended the Thirty
Years War in 1620, after prayers had been said to Our Lady. The
church was built earlier, but renamed to mark this event. Visitors
mostly come not because the church was originally built by Maderna,
rich though it is in coloured marble, but because it contains (left
transept) Bernini's famous statue of *St Teresa of Avila*, foundress of
the 16th century order of Reformed Carmelites. Bernini, as well

as being a sculptor, was also a theatrical producer, and has here given full rein to his dramatic talent, right down to the accompanying figures, who gaze in fascination from their opera boxes. But he has done no more than put into marble Teresa's own vivid description of her mystical union with Christ. While an angel (an Eros?) poises his arrow with a compassionate smile, Teresa swoons in ecstasy, her flowing robes as if on fire. Viewers differ in their reaction. Some are embarrassed, feeling themselves no more than *voyeurs* of this indescribable experience. Others simply marvel at the artist's superb skill and supreme control of his material.

> *Song 8: 3-4*: O that his left hand were under my head,
> and that his right hand embraced me!
> I adjure you, O daughters of Jerusalem,
> that you stir not up nor awaken my beloved
> until it please her.

MAUSOLEUM OF AUGUSTUS

Piazza Augusto, just off the Via del Corso.
Map E2. Entrance is free, but it tends to be closed.

Everybody knows the gigantic circular tomb which the emperor Hadrian built for himself and his family, because it stands so prominently on the Tiber bank, and is now known as the Castel S. Angelo (see p.44). The similar mausoleum which Augustus built over a hundred years earlier (27BC) stands in a back street and remains little known, in spite of being the tomb of a whole string of emperors (Caligula, Tiberius, Claudius, Nerva) headed by Augustus himself, in whose honour the month he was buried here has been called August ever since. It was converted into a fortress in mediæval times, and later into a concert hall, the **Augusteo**. Mussolini rescued it in 1936, and restored it to something of its former glory. Concentric corridors lead to the crypt in which the cremated emperors were laid.

Nearby, a little closer to the Tiber in the Via di Ripetta, is the **Ara Pacis**, a sacrificial altar commemorating the 'peace' and stability which the reign of Augustus brought to the feuding Roman Empire. It dates from 13BC and stands, appropriately enough, in the centre of the **Campus Martius**, the Field of the (war god) Mars (see p.41). This too was successfully restored by Mussolini in 1938, after archæologists had rescued the many fragments which had become part of the foundations of adjoining buildings, and recovered other pieces which had found their way to the museums of Florence and the Louvre. Protected now by glass, the delicate pyramidal marble altar is richly decorated with life-size reliefs.

Open 9.00-13.00 (Tues and Sat also 15.30-19.30). Closed Mon. Admission charge, except for under 18's and over 60's.

Luke 2: 1: In those days a decree went out from Caesar Augustus that all the world should be enrolled.

MAXENTIUS, CIRCUS of.
see p.33.

MEDICI VILLA
see p.119.

METHODIST CHURCH
see p.23.

MONTECAVALLO (Piazza del Quirinale)
see p.122.

MONTE TESTACCIO

Near the Porta S. Paolo. Map H2.

This strange little mountain on the banks of the Tiber, literally 'Crockery Hill', dates from the 1st century AD pottery jars in which wine, oil, honey, olives and grain used to be shipped from abroad to this wharf on the river. Rather than returning the empties, the dockers found it easier to ditch them. The result is a 45m mound made up entirely of potsherds, crowned eventually by a mediæval cross when local Lenten pageants used it as a Calvary. In more recent times numerous passages have been dug through the mound to provide several even-temperature cellars and wine shops. The adjoining area is famous for its moderately priced restaurants.

MONUMENT OF VICTOR EMMANUEL II

Piazza Venezia. Map F3.

There is almost nowhere in Rome from where this monument cannot be seen. Some people resent this, in something of the way that the Eiffel Tower in Paris is resented. They call it 'The Wedding Cake', and find it an eyesore, a vulgar intrusion among the hallowed stones of mellow antiquity. They are presumably unaware that those mellow stones were also once clad in white marble, and that in its heyday the whole of Rome gleamed as arrogantly as this building does. In erecting this monument to celebrate the newly won union of all the Italian states under a single king in 1870, the Romans were doing nothing other than what their forebears had always done. It is true that for a royal house which in the event survived the reign of only four kings, the monument is a bit of an overstatement. It is also true that the Brescian marble with which the monument is faced was commissioned by a prime minister who was the member for Brescia. But similar comments could be made about many of the monuments of imperial Rome.

The monument stands 70m high, and may soon be again open to the public as it was when it was first built. A magnificent flight of steps ascends to a statue of the goddess Roma, to whom her people come in procession to pay homage. At her feet is the tomb of an Unknown Warrior from World War I, attended at all times by guards. Above, stands the 12m equestrian statue of Victor Emmanuel, a little embarrassed (history tells us) that to achieve this eminence he had to drive pope Pius IX out of the Quirinal Palace, and make him a prisoner of the Vatican. Behind stands a massive colonnade, topped by winged Victories in their chariots. Inside the monument is a museum of archives. Outside, the view over Rome is one of the best.

The **Piazza Venezia** fronting the monument takes its name from the fine 15th century palace on its west side (to the right facing the monument), built from Colosseum stone by the Venetian cardinal who eventually became pope Paul II. During the 1930's the palace was used by Mussolini as his city office. It had a convenient balcony from which he frequently addressed the crowds in the spacious piazza below.

The adjoining **Church of St Mark**, originally a chapel for the palace, has some fine 9th century Byzantine mosaics. St Mark is said to have written his Gospel on this spot. In the porch, the oldest part of the church, there is to the right the tomb of the mistress of pope Alexander VI, mother of the notorious Cesare and Lucrezia Borgia.

Mark 1: 1-3:
The beginning of the gospel
of Jesus Christ, the son of God.
As it is written in Isaiah the prophet,
'Behold, I send my messenger before thy face,
who shall prepare thy way;
the voice of one crying in the wilderness:
Prepare the way of the Lord'.

MOUTH OF TRUTH (Bocca della Verità)

see p.89.

NATIONAL GALLERY

see p.35.

NATIONAL MUSEUM

see p.38.

NAVONA, Piazza.

Off the Corso Vittorio Emmanuele. Map EF2.

The word 'Navona' is a bowdlerisation of the *agones* or athletic contests which once took place in this 1st century stadium built by the emperor Domitian. The piazza has preserved exactly the elegant shape of the original (240m x 65m), though the houses now lining the sides were once tiers of seats for 30,000 people. The area was even at times flooded to allow naval battles (*naumachia*) to take place. Today it is a popular rendezvous for prodigal aperitif drinkers and street artists, and in December and January the site of an enormous children's fair, when the Epiphany Witch (*La Befana*) asks the children if they have been good.

The square is graced by three fountains, the central one a spectacular acrobatic feat by Bernini, who has balanced the old obelisk from the Via Appia (see p.33) on an apparent void. The statues beneath represent the great rivers of the Four Continents (Australia was not yet discovered) – the European Danube, the Asian Ganges, the African Nile and the American Plate – the latter two visibly shocked (it is said) by the façade of St Agnes, built by Bernini's rival Borromini.

The monumental **Church of St Agnes** dominates the piazza. Both inside and out, it is a fine example of the baroque style with which the 17th century popes commissioned artists to beautify Rome. It is said to be built on the site where a 4th century Christian girl, refusing to marry a governor of the city, was stripped naked in a brothel, miraculously grew knee-length hair, and was executed. She was buried in a Christian catacomb north of the city (see p.49). From the evidence of a skull reputed to be hers, she was aged 13. She continues to be commemorated in the list of saints in the Roman Canon of the Mass. There is a crypt with remains of the original seats which surrounded the stadium, and an altar with a 17th century bas-relief by Algardi.

Roman Canon of the Mass:
For ourselves, too, we ask
some share in the fellowship of your apostles and martyrs ...
with Felicity, Perpetua, Agatha, Lucy,
Agnes, Cecilia, Anastasia
and all the saints.
Though we are sinners,
we trust in your mercy and love.

G. Belli:

Se pò fregà	It can thumb its nose,
Piazza Navona mia	our Piazza Navona,
e de San Pietro	both at St Peter's
e de Piazza de Spagna.	and the Piazza di Spagna,
Questa nun è una piazza,	This is no piazza,
è una campagna,	we're in the country,
un treàto, una fiera,	it's a theatre, a fairground,
un'allegria.	sheer poetry. (*Piazza Navona*)

NEMI

see p.143.

OBELISKS OF ROME

❏ See p.102/ 103 for the Obelisks of Rome table

The passion for laying hands on these noble ancient monoliths, erected to celebrate the glories of the Egyptian pharaohs, and then laboriously *schlepping* them overseas, is illustrated not only by the obelisks now standing on London's Embankment and in Paris' Place de la Concorde, but even more recently by Mussolini's determination to show what a true successor he was of the ancient Roman emperors by hauling back a 24m stone from the holy city of Axum after 'conquering' Abyssinia in 1937, and installing it at the far end of the Circus Maximus.

But where London and Paris have only one obelisk to their name, Rome has thirteen. Under its clear sky, they remain as legible as on the day they were cut, unlike the grimy *Cleopatra's Needle* that broods over the Thames. Some of them (like that same *Needle*) date from the 14th or 15th century BC, and might have been seen in their pristine glory by our Israelite forebears when they were exiles in Egypt. Some are mere 'modern' reproductions, the foibles of Roman emperors wanting to glorify themselves. Many have stories attached, the most dramatic being that of the obelisk now in the centre of St Peter's Square (see p.110).

Those who rejoice that these ancient monuments still grace the

❏ Refer to
p.101 for the
Obelisks of
Rome entry

Date	Made in	For	Brought to Rome by	Date
BC1440	Karnak	Thutmosis III	Fl. Constantinus	AD 357
BC1300	Heliopolis	Ramses II	?	AD 1st c
BC1300	Heliopolis	Ramses II	?	AD 1st c
BC1300	Heliopolis	Ramses II	?	AD 1st c
BC1300	Heliopolis	Ramses II	Augustus	BC10
BC 590	Heliopolis	Psametticus II	Augustus	BC10
?	Heliopolis?	?	Caligula	AD 40
BC 580	Sais	Hophra	?	AD 1st c
?	?	?	Domitian?	AD 70?
?	?	?	Domitian?	AD 70?
AD 70	Egypt	Domitian	Domitian	AD 70
AD 130	Egypt	Hadrian	Hadrian	AD130
?	Rome	?	–	?

Obelisks of Rome: a chronology

Roman piazzas should offer a vote of thanks to pope Sixtus V, who managed to rescue one imperial obelisk from oblivion in each year of his short pontificate (1585-90), and re-settle it where we can continue to enjoy it today. The table above summarises the details.

ONOFRIO
see p.79.

OSTIA
see p.143.

PALATINE HILL

See plan on p.104. Open as the Forum (see p.66), from which there is access by the Arch of Titus. One ticket covers both sites. There is a secondary entrance which leads directly onto the hill from the Via S. Gregorio, 200m down from the Colosseum. Bookshop and toilets.

Of the traditional 'Seven Hills' (see p.125), the Palatine holds pride of place as the birthplace of Rome. The classical custom of reckoning dates 'From the Foundation of the City' (*Ab Urbe Condita*, or

Erected in	Transferred by	Date	To	Height
Circus Maximus	Sixtus V	AD1588	LATERAN	32m
Temple of Isis	Sixtus V	AD1588	Collegio Romano	
	Clement XI	AD1711	PANTHEON	5.5m
Temple of Isis	SPQR	AD1887	P. ESEDRA	5.5m
Capitol	Sixtus V	AD1590	VILLA CELIMONTANA	12m
Circus Maximus	Sixtus V	AD1589	PIAZZA DEL POPOLO	24m
Campus Martius	Pius VI	AD1792	MONTECITORIO	22m
Vatican	Sixtus V	AD1586	ST PETER'S SQ.	26m
Temple of Isis	Alexander VII	AD1667	MINERVA	5m
Maus. of Augustus	Pius VI	AD1682	QUIRINAL	14.5m
Maus. of Augustus	Sixtus V	AD1587	MARY MAJOR	14.5m
Temple of Isis	Maxentius	AD 309	Circus of Maxentius	
	Innocent X	AD1651	NAVONA	16.5m
Piazza Maggiore	Heliogabalus	AD 220	Circus Varianus?	
	Pius VII	AD1822	PINCIO	9m
Horti Sallustiani	Pius VI	AD1789	SPANISH STEPS	13m

A.U.C.) in the time of the legendary Romulus in 753BC has recently been vindicated by archæological evidence of an 8th century BC village built on this site. The hill, 500m high, forms a natural fortress, and is conveniently near to the Tiber island by which the river could be forded. It became most famous during imperial times, when first the Roman aristocracy, and then the emperors, built mansions for themselves on these cool heights above the sprawling city, and so bequeathed to the world the word by which every grandiose structure has been known ever since, a 'palatine building' or palace.

These buildings, like those in the Forum below, were superimposed on each other over the years, and during Rome's decay similarly used as a quarry. Mediæval lords built fortresses among these ruins, and Renaissance princes their villas. But these too have disappeared, though archæological excavations since the 18th century have brought much to light, and continue to do so. Some visitors may find it as difficult here, as in the Forum, to reconstruct mentally these ruined fragments into the imposing sights they once presented. Yet many find this unfrequented space more evocative of ancient Rome than the overcrowded Forum down below, and gladly take their picnics uphill among the shaded walks (beware litter). Those who need a visual aid to help them will get some idea of the Palatine's onetime grandeur by viewing its massive ramparts and arches from the **Circus Maximus** below (see p.52), especially at night time, when they are floodlit.

The gentle slope uphill from the Arch of Titus (**Clivus Palatinus**) leads, on the right, to a terrace with a casino overlooking the Forum. This is all that is left of the gorgeous villa which Vignola built in the 16th century for the Farnese family. But the **Farnese Gardens**, as they are still known (*Orti Farnesiani*) are still carefully tended, and the sophisticated cats who make their way up here from the Forum enjoy the roses and shrubbery as much as visitors do. The gardens cover the onetime lavish **Palace of Tiberius**, of which only a few stones remain. It was under Tiberius (14-37AD) that Jesus died. He was born in the reign of his predecessor Augustus (20BC-14AD) who built himself a far more modest structure on the hill's highpoint just beyond these ruins. Only the **House of Livia** (his wife) remains, protected by a shelter, which needs an attendant to allow access to its delicate frescoes.

To the left of this are the ruins of the Palatine's most ambitious project – a blockbusting palace which was meant to put all previous buildings in the shade. Not much is left of Domitian's **Domus Augustana** ('Imperial Palace' – 81-96AD), but the remains of the 160m stadium (an actual race-course or just a fanciful sunken garden?) show the scale on which he built. It is on the ruins of this

1. Theatre of
    Marcellus
2. S. Maria
    Cosmedin
3. Monument
4. Forum of
    J. Caesar
5. Mamertine
    Prison
6. Curia
7. B. Aemiliana
8. Lawrence
9. Cosmas &
    Damian
10. Maxentius
11. St Theodore
12. St Anastasia
13. House of Livia
14. Casino
15. Farnese Gardens
    (Palace of
    Tiberius)
16. St Sebastian
17. St Bonaventure
18. Villa Mills
    (Palace of
    Domitian)
19. Sept Severus
    (Belvedere)
20. Colosseum

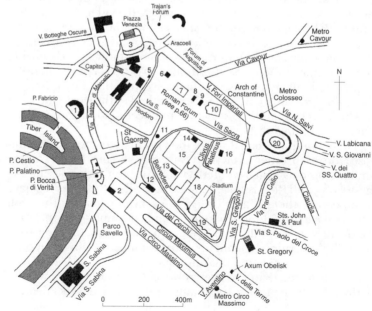

palace that the 19th century Scottish eccentric erected his gothic **Villa Mills,** pulled down in 1926 to give the archæologists access to the more important stones beneath.

The last Roman addition to the Palatine was made by the emperor who tried to subjugate the Scots 1700 years earlier. The **Palace of Septimius Severus** required massive arches to be built on the hillside before it could support his contribution to the splendours of the Palatine. These provide a fine *belvedere* or viewpoint over the Circus Maximus for the visitor who has wandered this far.

PALAZZOLA

see p.143.

PANTHEON

Map E3. Admission free, 9.00-17.00
(13.00 Sundays, 18.00 in winter).

This circular building (**La Rotonda**) is the only monument of ancient Rome to have survived more or less intact. The inscription on the porch attributes this temple 'of all the gods' (*pan-theon*) to M. Agrippa, son-in-law of Augustus in 27BC. But Agrippa's building was struck by lightning, and what we see today dates from a century later (all the bricks have the date 120AD stamped on them) under the emperor Hadrian (see **Castel S Angelo,** p.44 and **Tivoli,** p.145).

The dome, larger than that of St Peter's built 1500 years later, was the first ever made by the Romans. Cast in concrete in a single

piece, it was once plated in solid gold, as were the doors, but this has long since been pilfered. In fact the doors are fortunate to have survived at all: elsewhere the underlying bronze was either melted down in the mint, or appropriated for other buildings. Certainly the bronze that once covered the porch beams was removed in the 17th century by pope Urban VIII (Barberini) to forge into guns for his fortress at Castel S. Angelo, and (it is said) to form the elaborate pillars supporting the baldacchino in St Peter's – which evoked Pasquino's quip (see p.107): 'What the barbarians never descended to, the Barberini did'.

There were popes with quite another sense of priorities. When the catacombs were being raided for valuables by the 7th century barbarians, pope Boniface IV turned the abandoned Pantheon into a church, re-named it St Mary of the Martyrs, and brought there 28 cartloads of bones to be buried in the crypt.

Inside, the only light comes from the 10m aperture in the dome, casting an ethereal glow on the magnificent coffered ceiling. A sense of unity and perfect proportion is given by the diameter of the building, exactly equal to its height. The niches round the wall, designed for statues of the gods, have now become the tombs of Italy's kings (the Italians of Argentina even paid to have the piazza paved with wooden blocks instead of cobbles, to preserve a sacred silence here). Halfway along the wall on the left, low down, is the tomb of the artist Raphael, who was only 37 when he died in 1520. Devotees continue to bring flowers.

Outside, the sunken area around the building is alive with cats pleading to be photographed, the piazza with attractive cafés, and the side streets with an abundance of ecclesiastical suppliers.

Acts 17: 23-28:
(St Paul addresses the ancients and admires their deep sense of religion in putting up monuments to all *the gods, even the unknown ones):*
What you worship as unknown, this I proclaim to you. The God who made the world and everything in it, being Lord of heaven and earth, does not live in shrines made by man... He made from one every nation of men to live on all the face of the earth... that they should seek God, in the hope that they might feel after him and find him. Yet he is not far from each one of us, for 'In him we live and move and have our being', and 'We are indeed his offspring', as some of your poets have said.

Ille hic est Raphael, timuit quo sospite
vinci rerum Magna Parens, et moriente mori.
(Cardinal Bembo)

Living, great Nature feared he might outvie
her works, and dying, fears herself may die.
(trsl. Alexander Pope)

Michelangelo: No human being could have designed [the Pantheon]; it is the work of an angel.

PAPAL AUDIENCE
see p.24.

PARCO SAVELLO
see p.125.

PASQUINO

pasquinade: n. a lampoon or satire, originally one displayed in a public place (C.O.D. 1990).

This rare English word is taken from a Roman wit of the 16th century who called himself Pasquino, and who periodically stuck satirical epigrams on a dilapidated statue of Menelaus and Patrocles, still to be seen on the outside wall of the Palazzo Braschi in the tiny Piazza del Pasquino at the southern end of the Piazza Navona (Map F2). Fellow wits caught on, and would pin their responses and comments to the reclining figure of *Marforio* in the Capitol Museum (see p.43), and eventually onto a number of other ancient monuments. The custom ceased when journalism was invented. (See **Pantheon,** p.105 and **Quirinal**, p.122).

PATRICK, St
see p.23.

PAUL OUTSIDE THE WALLS, Basilica of St.
(S. Paolo fuori le mura)

Via Ostiense. Metro B, S. Paolo. Map L3.

Not all tourists to Rome bother to visit St Paul's: it lies isolated in an unattractive industrial area 2km outside the southern walls, and 4km from the city centre. But after St Peter's, it is the first place on the itinerary of every pilgrim, who has come to pray at the tombs of *the* apostles.

First impressions are disappointing, whether from the side entrance by the bus stop ('like a very ugly railway station' said the 19th century traveller Augustus Hare), or from the front, where the brash Victorian façade compares unfavourably with the mosaics of antiquity elsewhere in Rome. But all this is forgiven inside, where the visitor steps into a forest of 80 monumental granite columns set on a polished marble floor. The dim half-light from the high set alabaster windows bestows an atmosphere of silence, sacredness and awe. Ahead a noble arch frames the gothic canopy which stands over the high altar and the apostle's tomb. The basilica ends in the gentle glow of a mosaic apse. Many who find the baroque of most Roman churches too overpowering, here breathe a sigh of relief.

St Paul died a martyr's death about 67AD, and was buried in a cemetery outside the city on the Ostia road. In the 4th century Constantine built a chapel over the grave, and his successors extended this into a noble Roman basilica, 120m long and 23m high, the largest church in the world until the 16th century St Peter's was built. There was even a colonnade of 800 marble columns linking it with the walls of Rome.

All this has now disappeared, the basilica itself having been almost totally razed in a fire in 1823. What has been rebuilt around the 5th century triumphal arch (the sole survivor) is an exact copy of the five-aisled original, and it continues to give a clear picture of what the imperial basilicas in the Roman Forum once looked like. The apse mosaic (Christ attended by apostles) is a reconstruction of what the fire destroyed, and above the columns the small circular portraits of 265 popes have also been reconstructed. The 13th century canopy over the altar has been restored, and the transept contains a fine 12th century candelabrum. Beneath lies the tomb with the simple inscription, 'To Paul, Apostle and Martyr'.

Off the right transept is the entrance to the cloister. This 13th century marvel, with its rich and imaginative cosmati pillars, was mercifully spared in the conflagration, and is perhaps more attractive than any of those in the city. It marks the fact that we are on monastic ground: the attached monastery is the headquarters of the Benedictine Order.

2 Timothy 4: 6-8:
I am already on the point of being sacrificed; the time of my departure has come. I have fought the good fight, I have finished the race, I have kept the faith. Henceforth there is laid up for me the crown of righteousness, which the Lord, the righteous judge, will award to me on that Day, and not only to me but also to all who have loved his appearing.
(From a letter said to have been written by Paul from Rome about 66AD).

Thomas Merton:
We must never let our religious ideas, customs, rituals and conventions become more real to us than the Risen Christ. We must learn, with St Paul, that all these religious accessories are worthless if they get in the way of our faith in Jesus Christ, or prevent us from loving our brothers and sisters in Christ.

Paul looked back on the days when he had been a faultless observer of religious law, and confessed that all this piety was *meaningless*. He rejected it as worthless. He wanted one thing only. Here are his words:

I believe nothing can happen that will outweigh
the supreme advantage of knowing Christ Jesus my Lord.
For him I have accepted the loss of everything,

and I look on everything as so much rubbish,
if only I can have Christ and be given a place in him.
I am no longer trying for perfection by my own efforts,
but I want only the perfection that comes from faith in Christ.
All I want to know is Christ
in the power of his Resurrection
and to share his sufferings
by reproducing the pattern of his death.

(Philippians 3: 8-11)
He is Risen.

About 2km further south, close to the E.U.R (see p.64) is the monastery of **Tre Fontane** (Metro B, Laurentina), set in a former malarial valley now drained by eucalyptus trees. It is the traditional site of Paul's execution, where his head is said to have bounced three times to form three fountains (hence the name), but perhaps the springs were there before. Three small churches built here are in charge of Benedictine monks of the strictest observance, called Trappists. They have a small shop selling chocolate and eucalyptus liqueur.

Nearby, in a cave in the hillside, is a shrine known as **Our Lady of Revelation**, where an atheist bus driver caused a stir in 1947 by claiming a vision of Our Lady dressed (unusually) in green. It is served by Franciscan fathers.

PETER, Basilica of St. (S. Pietro)

Map E1.

As the gospels tell it, although Jesus chose twelve men 'to be with him' (Mark 3: 14) so that they could be 'sent out' (*apostoloi*) to preach what he had taught them, it was one of the twelve, Simon Peter, who acted as spokesman for the rest. Having boldly acclaimed Jesus as the Christ-Messiah whom the Jewish faith had longed for across the centuries, it was he who was charged to 'strengthen his brethren' (Luke 22: 31) and 'feed the flock' (John 21: 15-17). The office of the Roman papacy sees itself as continuing to fulfil that role. Jesus, we could say, was a vicar (stand in) for God. Peter was vicar of Christ. Popes are vicars of Peter.

Tradition tells us that Peter took the gospel to Rome, even before Paul arrived. For his pains he was executed in Nero's extramural circus built on the slopes of Vatican Hill, about 64AD, and buried nearby. When Constantine allowed Christianity to go public in the 4th century AD, he built a basilica in Peter's honour against the hillside. Several times restored and enlarged, this building eventually fell into disrepair, especially during the years in which the popes abandoned Rome for Avignon. On their return a worldwide appeal was launched for funds to erect a new one, not always by the most honest means (Chaucer and later Luther were loud in their protests, especially over the sale of indulgences). The new plan was 'to build the Pantheon [see p.105] on the Basilica of Maxentius' (see p.70). It took a hundred years and involved, one after another, all the great architects of the time: Bramante, Raphael, Sangallo junior, Michelangelo and Fontana. Before it was completed, the Borghese pope Paul V commissioned Maderna to increase the capacity by extending the nave of Michelangelo's four-square building and adding a façade. This unfortunately put the magnificent dome into the shade, but it allowed the pope to put his name on the front. The basilica was opened in 1626.

Once hidden behind the mediæval houses which clustered round it, St Peter's is now approached by the **Via della Conciliazione**, Mussolini's clumsy attempt in 1936 to give expression to the reconciliation between Church and State achieved in the Lateran Treaty of 1929 (his previous attitude is illustrated in his orders that no street in the Prati district, then being built, should have a view of St Peter's dome). This meant demolishing a whole row of picturesque buildings, but it allows a vista of St Peter's long before one reaches it.

The road opens onto the magnificent ellipse of the **Piazza S. Pietro**, perhaps based on the groundplan of the Colosseum, of which this is about twice the size, 340m by 240m. Bernini lined his piazza with a colonnade of 284 travertine columns, four deep, its central aisle wide enough for two carriages to pass each other. A disc set in the paving either side of the obelisk marks the focal point from which each row of four columns appears as only one. Two stately fountains 8m high, flank the central obelisk, which rises twice as high again. It originally marked the centre of Nero's circus, the spot where Peter died. The story of its move to this position by Fontana (Michelangelo had declined the job) had an interesting ending. The operation of raising it into position was so dangerous that silence was imposed on everyone under pain of death. At the last moment the ropes on the pulleys had no more purchase, until a sailor who knew his ropes cried out for water to be poured on them. The ropes contracted and the obelisk settled. The sailor was not only spared but given the exclusive rights to sell palms to Rome's apostolic palaces. The cost of the whole operation surprised the pope, who included the words 'shocking price' (*incredib. sumptu*) in the inscription on the base.

When the weather is right, weekly papal audiences are held in this piazza (see p.24). It was during one of these in May 1981 that an attempt was made on John Paul II's life. To the right of the piazza rises the **Vatican Palace** (see p.133). There are toilets and post offices for Vatican stamps halfway along the right colonnade, and also at the top end of the left colonnade, where there is a bookshop as well.

A broad flight of shallow steps, guarded by statues of St Peter and St Paul, leads up to the façade. It is from the balcony on top of this façade that the names of new popes are announced, and that the pope appears on festive occasions to pray for God's blessing on the city and the whole world (*urbi et orbi*). Inside the porch, the ceiling is elaborately decorated in stucco, and over the central entrance (facing out) can be seen one of the few remains of the earlier church, a heavily restored 14th century Giotto mosaic of *Peter's Ship in the Storm*. Three doorways lead into the basilica, the two on the left being recent works by Manzù, commissioned by pope John XXIII, who also set his coat-of-arms into the floor to commemorate the Second Vatican Council convened in 1962 under his pontificate.

The first sight of the interior is overwhelming by its sheer size. The very holy water stoups are like baths. 185m long and 46m high, capable of seating 60,000 people, the building yet retains a deep sense of proportion and harmony. A red circle of porphyry at the **entrance** (1) marks the spot where Charlemagne was crowned in 800AD, and so where the Roman Empire which had killed Jesus paradoxically became

Plan of St. Peter's

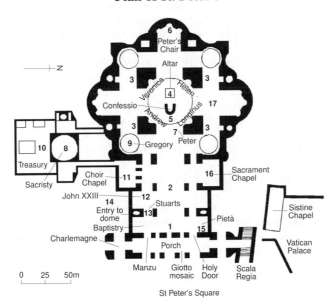

St Peter's Square

the Holy Roman Empire. Beyond, markers have been set into the floor to show how much smaller the world's other large churches are in comparison with this: Notre Dame of Paris, Santa Sophia in Constantinople, the cathedrals of Milan and Cologne, etc. London's St Paul's, though the largest of runners up, is rather chauvinistically given the title not of a church, but of a *fanum* – a (pagan) temple.

Visitors might do well to go from this entrance straight to the altar, in order to admire first what this building stands for: the rest of the details can be examined later. A short pause halfway up the **nave** (2) will give some idea of what Michelangelo's church would have looked like, the dome immediately visible on entry, with four equal arms leading from it. The dome is supported on four massive **piers** (3), in whose niches stand saints representing the relics enshrined here: St Helen's piece of the cross, St Veronica's veil, the centurion Longinus' lance, and St Andrew's head (only recently ecumenically returned to Greece from where the crusaders had looted it). Round the dome, on a golden frieze, in letters two metres high, runs the gospel text which proclaims Peter the rock on which the Church is built. Beneath the dome, sheltering the papal altar, stands the **canopy** (4) designed by Bernini at the age of 25, with its massive barley-sugar columns cast in bronze taken from the Pantheon (see p.105), copies of the ones with which Constantine had adorned Peter's tomb, but now the height of a Roman palace.

In front of the altar, a sunken space lit by oil lamps opens onto the **crypt** (5) in which St Peter is buried (see below), and before it lies a casket containing the *pallia* (neckbands) conferred on the new archbishops who will share in the pope's governance of the Church: a good place to kneel in prayer. Beyond this central altar, the apse is bathed in the gold of Bernini's alabaster window, before which he has suspended the remains of the **chair** (6) from which Peter is said to have taught (see p.120), encased in bronze and supported by others teachers (*doctors*) of the Church: Ambrose and Augustine in the west, Athanasius and Chrysostom in the east. At the base of the Longinus pier to the right is a **bronze statue of Peter** (7), a 13th century copy of a 5th century Greek teacher, whose feet are worn smooth by 700 years of kissing. The statue is robed and crowned on his feast day, 29th June.

Going back down the church by its left aisle, past papal monuments, several side altars (there are 29 of them altogether) and confessional boxes (the stick displayed outside like an aerial confers an indulgence), the entrance to the **Sacristy** is to the right (8). Outside is an **altar** dedicated to St Gregory the Great, apostle of England (9) (see p.76). Inside the entrance there is access to the **Treasury** (10), which contains a collection of precious objects, among them the so-called dalmatic of Charlemagne, and a maquette of Michelangelo's *Pietà* (see below) (open 9.00-18.30, 17.30 in winter. Admission charge). Further along is the **Choir Chapel** (11), in which the canons of St Peter sing the divine office daily. Its pride is Raphael's *Transfiguration*, but in mosaic, the original canvas (as in the rest of the basilica) having been transferred to the Vatican Museum for safe-keeping (see p.133). A chapel just beyond has **a bronze relief** in honour of Pope John XXIII (d. 1963) (12), and on the final pillar, left and right, **monuments** by Canova to the last of the English Stuarts who are buried in the crypt below – the Old Pretender ('James III'), and his sons Bonnie Prince Charlie and the cardinal Duke of York ('Henry IX') (13). English residents and pilgrims keep the monument supplied with roses. At this point there is to the right a stairway and a lift up to the **roof** (14).

The right aisle still needs to be explored. In the first side chapel is the famous **Pietà** (15), the dead Christ in the arms of his mother. It was carved by Michelangelo in 1500AD when he was only 24 (he even signed his name on the bandolier across Mary's breast), and remains a tribute to his monumental genius. It has been restored since the vandalism of 1972 and is now protected by bullet-proof glass. Copies of this masterpiece are popular in the shops, but are inevitably shoddy replicas.

C. Day Lewis:
A dome superb as heaven's vault, capping a story
Whose hero blessed the meek; a desert of floor
Refracting faith like a mirage; the orchestration
Of gold and marble engulfing the still, small voice:-
You cannot pass over St Peter's and what it stands for,
Whether you see it as God's vicarious throne
Or the biggest bubble yet unpricked …
I was lost, ill at ease here, until by chance

In a side chapel we found a woman mourning
Her son: all the *lacrimæ rerum* flowed
To her gesture of grief, all life's blood from his stone.
There is no gap or discord between the divine
And the human in that pieta of Michelangelo.

(An Italian Visit)

Further up the church, the **Blessed Sacrament Chapel** (16) has a 17th century tabernacle by Bernini, and a bronze grille designed by his rival Borromini. Finally we reach the **transept** again, the right wing of which (17) housed the 650 bishops who came here to argue the issues raised in the First Vatican Council in 1869, especially the controversial question of the pope's infallibility. The bishops who came to Vatican II in 1962 had increased to 3,000, and used the main nave.

The **Crypt** of St Peter's (**Grotte**) is entered by one of the four piers supporting the dome, the access differing according to demand. It is open from 7.00 till 18.00 daily (winter till 17.00) and the entrance is free. Below there are tombs of popes old and new, the oldest being that of the headless St Peter, the authenticity of which has satisfied the archæologists who searched the area for ten years between 1940 and 1950. Their excavations can be seen beneath the grilles in the floor, and are accessible only with permission. At floor level, pilgrims will be glad to pray at the tombs of Pius XII, John XXIII, Paul VI and John Paul I, and may even find the tomb of the only English pope, Adrian IV. The exit from the crypt does not lead back into the basilica, but out into the piazza. Toilets on the way.

The **Roof** of St Peter's can be reached by lift or by the 142 winding stairs which begin at the lower end of the church's left aisle (14). (Open 8.00-18.00, winter 17.00, admission charge). The roof offers a fine view across Rome, a café, post office, shops and toilets. The lift goes no further, and those who wish to go higher must do so on foot. From the top of the drum beneath the dome, there are vertiginous views of the interior of the church. The further ascent to the lantern involves a claustrophobic climb up 537 steps between the two shells of the dome (one has to stay aslant most of the way). From the lantern there is a ladder up into the ball, 133m above the ground, but the view is not better than it was below.

Matthew 16: 13-19:
When Jesus came into the district of Caesarea Philippi, he asked his disciples, 'Who do men say that the Son of man is?' And they said, 'Some say John the Baptist, others say Elijah, and others Jeremiah or one of the prophets'. He said to them, 'But who do you say that I am?' Simon Peter replied, 'You are the Christ, the Son of the living God'. And Jesus answered him, 'Blessed are you, Simon Bar-Jona! For flesh and blood has not revealed this to you, but my Father who is in heaven. And I tell you, you are Peter the rock, and on this rock I will build my church, and

the powers of death shall not prevail against it. I will give you the keys of the kingdom of The Heavens [God], and whatever you bind on earth shall be bound in heaven, and whatever you loose on earth shall be loosed in heaven.

John 18: 15-27:
Simon Peter followed Jesus... The maid who kept the door said to Peter, 'Are not you also one of this man's disciples?' He said, 'I am not'. Now the servants and officers had made a charcoal fire, because it was cold, and they were standing and warming themselves; Peter also was with them, standing and warming himself... They said to him, 'Are not you also one his disciples?' He denied it and said, 'I am not'. One of the servants... asked, 'Did I not see you in the garden with him?' Peter again denied it; and at once the cock crowed.

John 21: 15-17:
Jesus said to Simon Peter, 'Simon, son of John, do you love me more than these?' He said to him, 'Yes, Lord; you know that I love you'. He said to him, 'Feed my lambs'. A second time he said to him, 'Simon, son of John, do you love me?' He said to him, 'Yes, Lord, you know that I love you'. He said to him, 'Tend my sheep'. He said to him the third time, 'Simon, son of John, do you love me?' Peter was grieved because he had said to him the third time, 'Do you love me?' And he said to him, 'Lord, you know everything; you know that I love you'. Jesus said to him, 'Feed my sheep'.

St Bernard of Clairvaux:
What marvel if thou languish,
vigour and virtue fled,
wasted and spent with anguish,
and pale as are the dead?...
Spurn not a sinner's crying
nor from thy love outcast,
but rest thy head in dying
on these frail arms at last.
(Salve caput cruentatum, trsl. R.A. Knox)

Contemporary Prayers:
Heavenly Father,
help us like Peter
to trust you enough to obey you;
to follow though this will be to fail you;
to persist, that after our humiliation
we may hear you come again to bid us follow,
and our faith be then of rock that Satan cannot shift.

PETER IN CHAINS, Church of St.
(S. Pietro in Vincoli).

Entrance by steps up from Via Cavour. Metro B Cavour. Map F4.

This 5th century church is named after the piece of chain displayed in a glass casket under the high altar, a gift from pope Leo the

Great, said to be that with which St Peter was shackled in his Jerusalem prison, later miraculously joined to a second chain from his Mamertine prison (see p.86). Behind the altar are the reputed remains of the Maccabee martyrs (see below).

Few visitors come to see the Maccabees or even the chains. What draws the crowds is Michelangelo's monument to pope Julius II, patron of the Renaissance, in the right transept. A larger version of the monument was meant for St Peter's but was never achieved. One has to be grateful that this group of figures, particularly that of **Moses**, survives in a back street in Rome as a tribute to Michelangelo's genius. The Israelite leader is shown holding the tablets of the Ten Commandments he has just received from God on Mount Sinai, his face still radiant with his vision, but simultaneously enraged, his veins bursting, at the sight of the Golden Calf which has equivalently nullified God's first command. The combination of the two emotions is electric. When Michelangelo had finished the statue, he is said to have shouted at it to speak to him. All the Jews living in Rome at the time flocked to venerate it.

Mass tourism, by definition, attracts crowds. Writers of guidebooks bewail this, even though their sales figures have caused it. The fact remains that the monumental Moses is today often dwarfed by the crowds and the souvenir sellers. The Canons Regular of the Lateran, who look after the church, also have their own shop to the right, where there is an entrance to a 15th century cloister.

Exodus 32: 15-19:
Moses went down from the mountain with the two tables of the testimony in his hands... the work of God... As soon as he came near the camp and saw the calf and the dancing, Moses' anger burned hot, and he threw the tables out of his hands and broke them at the foot of the mountain.

Exodus 34: 34-35:
When Moses told the people of Israel what he was commanded, the people of Israel saw the face of Moses, that the skin of Moses' face shone [Vulgate, 'was horned', *a mistranslation*]; and Moses would put the veil upon his face, until he went in to speak with the Lord.

2 Corinthians 3: 7-18:
The Israelites could not look at Moses' face because of its brightness... He put a veil over his face so that the Israelites might not see the end of the fading splendour ... But when anyone turns to the Lord the veil is removed ... We all, with unveiled face, beholding the glory of the Lord, are being changed into his likeness from one degree of glory into another.

G. Vasari:
Michelangelo's design for the pope's tomb surpassed every ancient and imperial tomb ever made.

Acts 12: 2-10:
Herod killed James the brother of John with the sword; and when he saw that it pleased the Jews, he proceeded to arrest Peter also... He put him in prison, and delivered him to four squads of soldiers to guard him... So Peter was kept in prison; but earnest prayer for him was made to God by the church. The very night when Herod was about to bring him out, Peter was sleeping between two soldiers, bound with two chains, and sentries before the door were guarding the prison; and behold, an angel of the Lord appeared, and a light shone in the cell; and he struck Peter on the side and woke him, saying, 'Get up quickly.' And the chains fell off his hands... And he went out and followed him; he did not know that what was done by the angel was real, but thought he was seeing a vision... They came to the iron gate leading into the city. It opened to them of its own accord... And immediately the angel left him.

2 Maccabees 7: 1-41:
Seven brothers and their mother were arrested and were being compelled by the king [Antiochus IV Epiphanes 166BC] under torture with whips and cords, to partake of unlawful swine's flesh. One of them, acting as their spokesman, said... 'We are ready to die rather than transgress the laws of our fathers.' The king fell into a rage, and gave order that pans and cauldrons be heated. These were heated immediately, and he commanded that the tongue of their spokesman be cut out and that they scalp him and cut off his hands and feet, while the rest of the brothers and mother looked on... The brothers and their mother encouraged one another to die nobly, saying, 'The Lord God is watching over us and has compassion on us... The King of the universe will raise us up to an everlasting renewal of life, because we have died for his laws...' The mother was especially admirable. Though she saw her seven sons perish within a single day, she bore it with good courage, because of her hope in the Lord... Last of all, the mother died, after her sons.

PETER IN MONTORIO, Church of.
see p.80.

PIAZZA BARBERINI
see p.36.

PIAZZA COLONNA
see p.55.

PIAZZA DEL POPOLO
see p.94.

PIAZZA DI SPAGNA

Map E3.

Spain has stolen this famous piazza's name. It belongs by right to the French, who paid for the glorious flight of steps joining the piazza to the French church on the Pincio hill above. The Spanish name comes from the Spanish embassy to the Vatican, which has been situated at the narrow end of the piazza since the 17th century, and since 1854 graced with the grandiose column commemorating the definition of the Immaculate Conception of Mary. Each year on 8th December the Roman Fire Brigade renew the wreath on Mary's head, and the pope comes to pay his respects.

Even without the flight of steps, the piazza is a joy, providing a delightful breathing space after the many streets of fashionable shops that converge on it. It is always alive with umbrella'd flower sellers, who refresh their plants from the gentle central **Barcaccia fountain** ('The Old Tub'), designed by Bernini. The area has long been a favourite with English visitors, who knew it as the West End of Rome. It was they who set up the 1896 **Babington Tea-rooms** on the left of the steps, still going strong and still expensive; and on the right, the **Keats Memorial House and Library**, where the poet died in 1821 (open 9.00-13.00, 15.00-18.00, winter 14.30-17.30, admission charge). But other nationalities have also been attracted to the area, which remains an active artists' quarter. The **Caffè Greco** in Via Condotti 86 still remembers Byron, Goethe, Nietzsche, Liszt and Wagner, when the price of a coffee at the gilt and marble-topped tables was not as prohibitive as it is today.

But it is, of course, the exuberant **Steps** which since 1723 have made this piazza unique in Rome. Sweeping up in elegant curves, dividing and rejoining twice, they have always been a meeting place for friends to sit together, especially the young. These add considerable colour to the scene, which becomes almost a riot when the spring azaleas come into bloom.

At the top of the steps stands the twin-towered church of the **Trinità dei Monti**, with a fine 16th century *Deposition from the Cross* in the second chapel on the left. Attached is a convent of the Sacred Heart Sisters, famous for offering hospitality to Cornelia Connelly, foundress of the Loreto or Mary Ward nuns (IBVM), and for a botched painting of the Madonna (*Mater Admirabilis*), which is said to have miraculously become more photogenic overnight. St Thérèse of Lisieux prayed here.

The obelisk in front of the church is a fake with imitation hieroglyphs, made in Rome not in Egypt.

Pius IX:
We declare, pronounce and define that this doctrine – that the most Blessed Virgin Mary was, from the first moment of her conception, through a singular privilege freely bestowed by Almighty God, and in the view of the merits of Jesus, Saviour of the human race, preserved immune from all stain of original sin – has been revealed by God, and therefore must be firmly and unwaveringly believed by all the faithful. (Bull *Ineffabilis Deus*, 8th December 1854)

PIAZZA DEL ESEDRA
see p.37.

PIAZZA NAVONA
see p.100.

PIAZZA S. PIETRO
see p.110.

PIAZZA VENEZIA
see p.99.

PINCIO GARDENS

Metro A, Flaminio. Map D3.

Napoleon's architect Valadier designed both the Piazza del Popolo and these gardens rising above it. Their walks, lined with busts of national heroes, provide a popular strolling area for Romans, especially in the evening. The view across the city from the western terrace is a magnificent one, and best of all at sunset. In summer a band plays in the gardens each Sunday evening.

To the south east, the gardens continue at a panoramic height above the city, and eventually reach the **Medici Villa** just before they end above the Piazza di Spagna. The 16th century villa itself, once the property of the Medici family, has since Napoleon's time been the home of the French Academy, and private art shows are held here from time to time. It is open to the public only on Wednesdays, 9.00-11.00. In the beautiful gardens at the back, Velàsquez did two of his paintings while Galileo was imprisoned inside for three years by the Inquisition.

POMPEY, THEATRE of.
see p.40.

POPOLO, Piazza and Porta del.
see p.94.

PRAXEDES (Prassede) and PUDENZIANA, Churches of Sts.

Both near St Mary Major. Map F4.

In the Via Urbana, below street level, is the very early church of St Pudenziana, dating from the 4th or early 5th century, and though much restored, still displaying its pre-Byzantine mosaic in the apse – Christ with the apostles Peter and Paul, who are being crowned with wreaths by two women. The Gentile and Jewish churches? Pudenziana and Praxedes? Who knows. (Use the slot machine to illuminate it).

There is a tradition that we are here on the site of the 2nd century house of a Roman senator named Pudens. There is a Roman of this name in the second epistle to Timothy (see below). Is it the same? If so, could he have acted as host to St Peter when he was in Rome? Pudens is said to have had two daughters, Pudenziana and Praxedes, though nothing whatever is known of them. Yet the tradition was strong enough for a chair found here to be encased in gold and hung high in the apse of St Peter's, and an accompanying table to be incorporated into the altar of the Lateran. (A small piece remains behind the glass in which cardinal Wiseman, then the church's protector, framed it).

The sister church of St Praxedes (S. Prassede) lies on the Via S. Martino ai Monti, just the other side of Mary Major's. It is also an early Christian foundation. In 817AD the pope had 2,300 bodies from the catacombs buried here (see p.47). Its apse mosaics, though later and so more hieratic (9th century), are among the finest in Rome: Peter and Paul with their arms around the same two women. Before it, on the arch, a scene from the book of Revelation, as in Sts Cosmas and Damian (see p.59). The chapel of St Zeno, near the entrance, also has exquisite mosaics, wall to wall, as well as part of a pillar brought here from Jerusalem, said to have been used for the scourging of Jesus in Pilate's palace. Since it is made of a rare marble (jasper), this is unlikely. But it makes a good visual aid. The sacristy has a shop.

2 Timothy 4: 21-22:
Greet Prisca and Aquila ... Eubulus sends greetings to you, as do *Pudens* and Linus and Claudia and all the brethren. The Lord be with your spirit. Grace be with you.
(Written from Rome in 66AD).

John 18: 38-19: 5:
Pilate went out to the Jews and told them, 'I find no crime in him'...
They cried out, 'Not this man, but Barabbas!' Now Barabbas was a
robber. Then Pilate took Jesus and scourged him. And the soldiers
plaited a crown of thorns, and put it on his head, and arrayed him in
a purple robe; they came up to him, saying, 'Hail, King of the Jews!' and
struck him with their hands. Pilate went out again, and said to them,
'See, I am bringing him out to you, that you may know that I find no
crime in him'. So Jesus came out, wearing the crown of thorns and the
purple robe. Pilate said to them, 'Behold the man!'

PRISCILLA, St
see p.49.

PROTESTANT CEMETERY
see p.39.

PUDENZIANA, St
see p.120.

PYRAMID
see p.39.

QUATTRO CORONATI, Church of.

Via dei Santi Quattro, near St Clement's.
Map G4.

This church, hidden in a back lane yet dominating the locality like
a small fortress, dates from the 4th century, though the present
building with monastery attached is from the 12th century. A totally
untraceable tradition has linked it with four (*quattro*) Roman
stonemasons who refused to pay honour to the pagan gods, and
were martyred. A vision of them with crowns of glory (*coronati*)
assured the visionary they were with God. Sculptors continue to
regard them as their patrons.

A bell tower and two courtyards lead to the church, which is
paved with cosmati work, and has an apse decorated with a 17th
century fresco of the Cross. To the left there is an entrance to the
charming 13th century two-storeyed cloister, with its graceful
fountain. At a small stall, the enclosed Canonesses of St Augustine,
who care for deaf and dumb children, sell postcards.

The church's main attraction is the chapel of St Sylvester on the
left of the inner courtyard as you leave. Ring at the convent door for
the key, delivered on a turntable, and return it with an offering

after. The chapel glows with its remarkably well-preserved 13th century frescoes of the pope who is said to have cured Constantine of his leprosy, and made a (sort of) Christian out of him. There is a fine *Last Judgement* over the door.

The churches of St Clement (p.52) and S. Stefano Rotondo (p.126) are near, and they could conveniently be visited at the same time.

John 12: 24:
Truly, truly, I say to you,
unless a grain of wheat
falls into the earth, and dies,
it remains alone;
but if it dies,
it bears much fruit.

QUIRINAL PALACE

Map E3.

The Quirinal hill is the highest of the traditional 'Seven' (see p.125), and became residential soon after the Roman forefathers ventured forth from their original Palatine hill. The poet Martial lived here in the 1st century AD and called it 'living in the country while still in town' (*rus in urbe*), but still complained of the noise, as people continue to do today.

Because of its fresh air, the 16th century popes commissioned Fontana, Maderna and Bernini to provide a summer villa for them up here, and they warmed to it so much that they soon forsook the less salubrious Vatican and took permanent residence. For 300 years, papal conclaves and the election of new popes took place in this palace. Another was built in the 18th century at right angles to it, to house the papal consultative court. It was only in 1870, with the advent of Italy's first king Victor Emmanuel II, and the abolition of the papal states, that the pope (Pius IX) returned to the Vatican, to become its 'prisoner'.

This, then was Italy's Buckingham Palace from 1870 to 1946. Since the end of the monarchy, it has been the official residence of Italy's president, and the palace opposite has become the Supreme Court. Neither is open to the public, but there is a colourful and musical changing of the guard every day about 16.00.

The **Piazza del Quirinale** (or **Montecavallo**) is one of Rome's delights. Enclosed on three sides, the fourth opens onto a comprehensive and magnificent panorama of the city. At the centre of the piazza stands a fountain, and a noble obelisk flanked by the legendary twin heroes Castor and Pollux (the same as guard the Capitol, see p.43), reining in two massive horses, ancient Roman copies (remarkably surviving unharmed) of the famous Greek originals. When they were put here by pope Pius VI in 1775, they were inscribed with the names of the sculptors Phidias and Praxiteles. But since he had changed the figures from an original position of facing the horses and checking them as they rear, to their present position beside the horses and pulling them back, the wag Pasquino (see p.106) drew attention to the aesthetic blunder by changing the words *Opus Phidiae* to *Opus perfidiae Pii Sexti*. The statue of Apollo which forms the monument to the Duke of Wellington in London's Hyde Park is based on the same figures.

QUO VADIS (Domine Quo Vadis, Church of)

see p.61.

REPUBBLICA, Piazza

see p.37.

ROCCA DI PAPA

see p.142.

SABINA, Church of St.

Via di S. Sabina on the Aventine. Map G3.

Many visitors to Rome vote this their favourite church. However hard they have tried to appreciate the baroque and rococo styles of other Roman churches, they feel that the majestic simplicity of this place puts them all in the shade.

Sabina is said to have been a 2nd century widow converted by her maidservant to Christianity, for which both were martyred. In the 5th century her house was turned into a church, one of the most graceful of the early Christian basilicas, with 24 noble marble columns rescued from the neglected classical buildings, and a screened and marbled choir. It is to this stark yet harmonious unity that the church has successfully been restored this century, the only decoration being the 5th century mosaic above the entrance of two figures representing the Church made up of Jews and Gentiles, and Sassoferrato's masterpiece of 1643 in the left aisle, *Our Lady of the Rosary*. The church has been in the care of the Dominican Fathers since the time of their founder in the 13th century, and continues on Ash Wednesday to head the list of the **Lent Stations** (see p.168) traditionally attended by the pope.

ECCLESIA EXCIR
CVMCLSIONE

In the spacious porch, the main door of the church is worth inspecting. It is made of cypress wood, and its panels of scenes from the Old and New Testament, carved in the 5th century, are some of the oldest examples of Christian art. The panel of the crucifixion has become famous. A peep-hole has been cut into the stone wall opposite to let people see an orange tree, descendant of the one planted here 700 years ago by St Dominic. Outside, stairs lead up into the monastery, where St Thomas Aquinas stayed when he visited Rome, and where the present Master is an Englishman, Timothy Radcliffe. There is a worthwhile souvenir shop at the entrance.

St Dominic:
Those who govern their passions are the masters of the world.
They must either rule them, or be ruled by them.
It is better to be the hammer than the anvil.

Ephesians 2: 11-14 (NJB):
Do not forget that there was a time when you gentiles, termed 'the uncircumcised' by those who speak of themselves as 'the circumcised', were separate from Christ and excluded from membership of Israel, aliens with no part in the covenants of the Promise, limited to this world, without hope and without God. But now in Christ Jesus, you that used to be so far off have been brought close, by the blood of Christ. For he is the peace between us, and has made the two into one entity, and broken down the barrier which used to keep them apart.

Adjoining S. Sabina, a little further up the road, is the church of **St Alexis (Alessio)**, which commemorates the strange story of a young Roman nobleman so sickened by his rich lifestyle that he left his bride on the wedding night to spend 17 years in Syria as a hermit. He then returned and spent another 17 years under the stairs of his family home as a servant, unrecognised even by his wife until she read a letter held in his dead hand. There is a monument to him just inside the church. Perhaps they should have put up one for his wife as well.

Next to this church is the **Priory of the Knights of Malta**. The lovely Piranesi piazza outside is frequently choked with coaches ever since someone accidentally peeped through a keyhole in the garden door and got a stunning view of St Peter's at the end of an avenue of trees. This **Keyhole View** has become a 'must' on all package tours of Rome. The view is indeed a worthwhile one, but the same vista of St Peter's (without the avenue) can be had more comfortably further back down the road from the elegant public **Parco Savello** with its delightful orange trees.

Just a few steps further on, the Aventine hill comes to an end in the **College of St Anselm**, the house of the Benedictine Order, and the residence of the Abbot Primate. The church is a replica of Rome's many basilicas from the year 1900, and is popular with liturgists for its singing. In the porch is a bronze of the Benedictine saint, Anselm, archbishop of Canterbury in the 11th century, and in the crypt an impressive modern statue of St Benedict.

> *From the Rule of St Benedict*:
> The leader of a community should temper all things, so that the strong may still have something to work for, and the weak may not give up hope.
> Working is a way of praying.
> The saying is that monks ought not to drink wine. But since today no monk believes this, let us at least drink in moderation.

SCALA SANTA (Holy Stairs)
see p.83.

SEBASTIAN, Catacomb of St.
see p.48.

SEVEN CHURCHES
see p.174.

SEVEN HILLS

> The note redouble till it fills
> With echoes sweet the Seven Hills.

An older generation will recall these lines of Wiseman's rousing hymn *Full in the panting heart of Rome*. He had picked up a description dating back to ancient Rome, when it was the heights to the east of the navigable Tiber that the earliest settlers picked upon to turn into a city in the 8th century BC: first the **Palatine** and **Capitoline** enclosing the Forum, and later the encircling **Quirinal** (Quirinal Palace), **Viminal**, **Esquiline** (Mary Major), **Coelian** (St Clement, Lateran) and **Aventine** (S. Sabina).

The rather higher hills of the Pincio to the north, and the Vatican and Janiculum to the west, were not settled until the time of Augustus (BC-AD), but were eventually also included in the walled city.

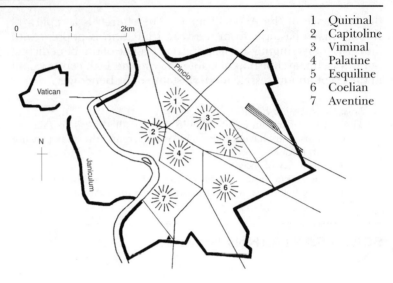

1 Quirinal
2 Capitoline
3 Viminal
4 Palatine
5 Esquiline
6 Coelian
7 Aventine

Map of the Seven Hills

SISTINE CHAPEL
see p.136.

SPADA PALACE
see p.41.

SPAGNA, Piazza di
see p.118.

SPANISH STEPS
see p.118.

STEPHEN IN THE ROUND, Church of St. (S. Stefano Rotondo)

Via di S. Stefano. Toilets. Map G4.

This 5th century church in honour of the protomartyr Stephen was originally constructed in the shape of three concentric circular aisles. In the 16th century a wall was built inside the outer one, making it far smaller. Moreover, the cross, which once intersected these circles, was eliminated. In spite of these rather drastic changes, the church retains a powerful sense of atmosphere, even more so after its recent restoration. It has a stillness and simple dignity which not all churches achieve.

When the 16th century wall was built, it was decorated with contemporary frescoes telling the story of the many martyrs who have followed the lead of Stephen through the ages. They are agonisingly explicit, and mutilation vies with impalation, boiling with skinning alive, roasting with crucifixion, to bear witness to the perennial inhumanity (and the perennial courage) of the human race. The English College (see p.63) tells the story of the English Martyrs in a choir loft decorated in a similar style, though 300 years later.

Since the church belongs to the German-Hungarian College in Rome, it venerates the memory of St Stephen of Hungary as well as that of the protomartyr. Within easy walking distance are the churches of St Clement (p.52) and Quattro Coronati (p.121).

Acts 7: 55-60:
Stephen, full of the Holy Spirit, gazed into heaven and saw the glory of God, and Jesus standing at the right hand of God; and he said, 'Behold, I see the heavens opened, and the Son of man standing at the right hand of God.' But they cried out with a loud voice and stopped their ears and rushed together upon him. Then they cast him out of the city and stoned him; and the witnesses laid down their garments at the feet of a young man named Saul. And as they were stoning Stephen, he prayed, 'Lord Jesus, receive my spirit.' And he knelt down and cried with a loud voice, 'Lord, do not hold this sin against them.' And when he had said this, he fell asleep.

P. Jacob:
Blessed are the poor
    not the penniless, but those whose heart is free.
Blessed are those who mourn
    not those who whimper, but those who raise their voices.
Blessed are the meek
    not the soft, but those who are patient and tolerant.
Blessed are those who hunger and thirst for justice
    not those who whine, but those who struggle.
Blessed are the merciful
    not those who forget, but those who forgive.
Blessed are the pure in heart
    not those who act like angels, but those whose life is transparent.
Blessed are the peacemakers
    not those who shun conflict, but those who face it squarely.
Blessed are those who are persecuted for justice
    not because they suffer, but because they love.
                  (Baptist Missionary Society, August 1985)

SUSANNA, St
see p.23.

SWISS GUARD

Since the Lateran Treaty of 1929 the Pope retains the right to maintain an armed force. Its present total strength is 120 trained soldiers from the Catholic cantons in Switzerland, armed only with halberds. But then who would today dream of attacking a pope?

Their colourful orange, blue and red uniform is said to have been designed by Michelangelo, at a time when slashed clothing was coming into fashion. To the delight of photographers, the fashion has never been changed since.

SYLVESTER, Church of St.

Off the Via del Tritone. Map E3.

Originally a monastic foundation, the monastery of St Sylvester has for long been converted into Rome's busy General Post Office. But the church remains, dedicated to the 4th century pope who made a Christian of Constantine in 314AD, and now served by the Pallottine Fathers for the English Catholics living in Rome. The church has been graced with the suffix *in capite* because it keeps what is reputed to be the head of St John the Baptist in a dark chapel on the left. Since that relic is also claimed to be in the principal mosque in Damascus, gullible pilgrims have been known to accept the explanation that one is the head of the saint when he was a young man.

> *Mark 6: 17-29*: Herod had sent and seized John, and bound him in prison for the sake of Herodias ... Herodias had a grudge against him, and wanted to kill him ... An opportunity came when Herod gave a banquet ... and Herodias' daughter came in and danced and pleased Herod and his guests ... And he vowed to her, 'Whatever you ask I will give you, even half of my kingdom'. And she went out, and said to her mother, 'What shall I ask?' And she said, 'The head of John the Baptiser'. And she came in immediately with haste to the king, and asked, saying, 'I want you to give me at once the head of John the Baptist on a platter'. And the king was exceedingly sorry; but because of his oaths and his guests he did not want to break his word to her. And immediately the king sent a soldier of the guard and gave orders to bring his head. He went and beheaded him in the prison, and brought his head on a platter, and gave it to the girl; and the girl gave it to her mother. When his disciples heard of it, they came and took his body, and laid it in a tomb.

SYNAGOGUE
see p.74.

TARPEIAN ROCK
see p.44.

TERME, see BATHS
p.36 and p.37.

THEATRE OF MARCELLUS
see p.87.

THEATRE OF POMPEY
see p.40.

TIBER ISLAND (Isola Tiberina)

Map F3.

The Ponte Fabricio leading from left-bank Rome to Trastevere is the oldest bridge in Rome, built in 62BC. Downstream it looks disdainfully at the arches of a bridge built a hundred years earlier but still a ruin (**Ponte Rotto**) despite numerous attempts to repair it. Halfway across to Trastevere, we are on the boat-shaped Tiber Island, looking for all the world like a mediæval castle sailing down the river.

The island has been dedicated to healing ever since 291BC, when a serpent (symbol of Aesculapius, god of healing) was seen swimming onto the island. A temple was erected to the god, and an infirmary attached. The tradition still continues in the hospital of the Brothers of St John of God, here called the *Fatebenefratelli* ('Do-gooders'), which occupies most of the island; and in the neighbouring 12th century **Church of St Bartholomew**, where an English Augustinian monk received a vision inspiring him to found a church in London, with a St Bart's hospital attached. The Roman church is reputed to have the body of the apostle Bartholomew, but Benevento claims the same.

A well-head in the choir of the island church is said to stand on the site of the pagan spring, and to contain curative waters.

John 5: 2-17:
There is in Jerusalem a pool ... where lay a multitude of invalids, blind, lame, paralysed. One man was there, who had been ill for thirty-eight years. When Jesus saw him and knew that he had been lying there a long time, he said to him, 'Do you want to be healed?' The sick man answered him, 'Sir, I have no man to put me into the pool when the water is

troubled, and while I am going another steps down before me.' Jesus said to him, 'Rise, take up your pallet, and walk.' And at once the man was healed, and he took up his pallet and walked ... Jesus said, 'My Father is working still, and I am working.'

(A gospel story associated with a spring dedicated to the same god Aesculapius)

TIBER, River (Tévere)

After the river Po, the 350km Tiber is Italy's longest river. Rising in the same part of the Apennines as the Rubicon, and emptying into the Mediterranean at Ostia (The Mouth), it is over 100m wide as it runs north to south through Rome in two great S-bends, leaving a small island in the middle of its course. Within the city it is spanned by fifteen bridges. It is perhaps most photogenic at the Island (map F4) and at Castel S. Angelo (map E2).

Legend has it that the river bed contains the treasures taken from the Jerusalem Temple by Titus, and flung here in 70AD. No-one has ever dredged the river to check this.

TIVOLI

see p.145.

TORTOISE FOUNTAIN (Fontana delle Tartarughe)

Map F3.

Anyone on foot in the area of Piazza Argentina should make the short detour to the Piazza Mattei to see one of Rome's most enchanting fountains, dating from the 16th century. Four strapping lads grasp dolphins, from whose mouths water pours into shells. The tortoises drinking from the fountain, although they have given their name to the fountain, were how-ever later additions.

H.V. Morton:
Rome is a city of magic round the corner, of masterpieces dumped, as it were, by the wayside, which lends to the shortest walk the excitement of a treasure hunt.

(A Traveller in Rome, 1957)

TRASTEVERE

Map FG2.

The semi-circle of Rome enclosed by the lower of the river's two S-bends was known from ancient times as *Transtiberina*, 'Across the Tiber'. Although it was included in the 3rd century walls, it continued until the 14th century to be regarded as a suburb of Rome rather than as part of the city, and its inhabitants were thought of as foreigners.

Far from being piqued by such ostracism, the Trasteverini are proud to call themselves *noialtri* ('we're different'), and make a festival of the fact each 15th-24th July. They regard themselves in fact as the lineal descendants of the ancient Romans, and all the left-bankers as upstarts. The cockneys of Rome, they have their own dialect, immortalised by their 19th century poet Belli, now resplendent in frock coat and top hat at the entrance of Trastevere's only main road. The rest is a maze of alleys, lanes and piazzas, rich in workshops, cafés and churches (see **Cecilia**, p.50, and **Maria in Trastevere**, p.95). It remains the most picturesque, almost theatrical, part of Rome, and its restaurants are famed.

There is a flea-market every Sunday morning at the Porta Portese, at the southern end of Trastevere.

TRE FONTANE
see p.109.

TREVI FOUNTAIN (Fontana di Trevi)

Halfway along Via del Corso, to the east. Map E3.

The 1950's film *Three Coins in the Fountain*, with its memorable theme song, has made this one of the most visited places in Rome, and the money regularly fished out of its basin bears witness to the popularity of the saying that anyone who throws a coin in this fountain (over the shoulders is suggested as the most effective) will return to Rome.

Its cramped setting in the tiny piazza adds dramatic effect to this spectacular fountain (best seen floodlit in the evening) designed, it is thought by Bernini, to enliven the outside wall of the renaissance Palazzo Poli. It was completed in 1762, the architect Salvi having died of pneumonia from the years he had spent underground in the aqueduct. It brings the pure waters of the Acqua Vergine (which also feeds the fountain in the Piazza di Spagna, see p.118) to the centre of Rome. The water-god Neptune presides triumphantly over the roar of a dozen cool waterfalls, prouder than ever since the recent cleaning of the whole façade (1992).

TRINITÀ DEI MONTI
see p.118.

TRITON FOUNTAIN
see p.36.

VATICAN CITY

Map E1.

Several Italian provinces were first bequeathed to the pope by Charlemagne's father Pepin in the 8th century AD. These 'Papal States' remained under the more or less undisputed rule of popes for a thousand years, until Napoleon made them part of his French Empire in the 19th century. They were restored for a short while, but when all the Italian states agreed to unite under a single king in 1870, the papal states, with their population of 3 million, were finally confiscated, and popes restricted to the Vatican, of which they called themselves the 'prisoners'. The 1929 Lateran Treaty confirmed the pope as sovereign of the Vatican, with extraterritorial rights over the major basilicas (St Paul, St Mary Major and the Lateran) and Castel Gandolfo.

The Vatican is the smallest state in the world, with an area of a mere 50,000m², the size of a good golf course, bounded by the Leonine Walls (Leo IV, 9th century). The pope is officially the Head of State, though affairs are administered by a Governor, and there is a cardinal Secretary of State. A thousand residents are protected by an army of 100 men (see Swiss Guards p.128) and a small police force. The state has its own flag, currency (parallel to the Italian lira), postal-telephone-telegraph service, radio station (35 languages), railway station (white marble), helipad, newspapers (the *Osservatore Romano* has 70,000 readers), and a fleet of 100 cars. The distinctive SCV number plates of the latter (*Sancta Civitas Vaticana*, The Holy City of the Vatican) has often been ironically transposed into *Se Cristo Vedesse* (If Only Christ Could See Us Now). There are guided bus tours of the grounds at 10.00 on Mon, Tues, Fri and Sat. Previous booking. Admission charge sizeable.

The extensive **Vatican Palace** has grown year by year ever since the popes returned from the Avignon exile in the 14th century. It now has 1400 rooms. Its main entrance is at the **Bronze Doors** at the end of the right hand colonnade in St Peter's Square, and it is here that private audiences with the pope are arranged. In recent years the palace has largely been turned over to the public as a museum. The entrance to this is now a kilometre away. A shuttle bus runs regularly every day (except Wed and Sun) from the **Information Office** (end of the left hand colonnade) to the museum entrance (see below).

A visitor: Your Holiness, can you tell me how many people work in Vatican City?
Pope John: About half.

VATICAN MUSEUM

Metro A, Ottaviano. Map E1.
Admission charge. Open 8.45 till 17.00
(Sat and winter only till 14.00). Closed Sun,
except the last Sun in the month, when entrance
is free, and crowds most dense. In high season,
it may be advisable to visit late rather than early.
Shorts and bare arms are forbidden.

There are 70 museums in Rome. This is by far the most popular, receiving a million and a half visitors a year. The galleries, which enclose two enormous courtyards of the Vatican Palace, contain 7km of displays and cannot possibly be appreciated in a single visit. But even the casual visitor cannot fail to be impressed by the wealth of art treasures which over the centuries have been amassed or commissioned by, or donated to, the popes, and admire a few of the highlights.

The entrance to the museum (1) is in the Viale Vaticano, at the end of the Vatican Palace, the furthest removed (1km) from St Peter's (map D1). A bus runs a regular shuttle service from the Piazza S. Pietro. The ticket office leads to a modern double spiral ramp (to ensure one-way traffic) which takes one to the top of the hill on which the palace is built. Here there is a shop, a money exchange and (in the courtyard) toilets, a sizeable restaurant (2), and a fine view of St Peter's. From this point, coloured itineraries suggest long and short routes through the museum. Human concentration being limited, many visitors would be well advised to follow the signs making straight for the **Sistine Chapel** at the far end of the museum, and ignore everything else as a distraction for the time being, hoping to catch the flavour of some of what they have missed later, by returning to the entrance and starting again. In the pages that follow, exhibits are listed in order of appearance.

Off the courtyard mentioned above is the 1932 *Pinacoteca* or **Picture Gallery** (3). The collection was first formed in 1815, when Napoleon returned (some of) the paintings he had stolen from Rome's churches. To these have been added a further 200 paintings

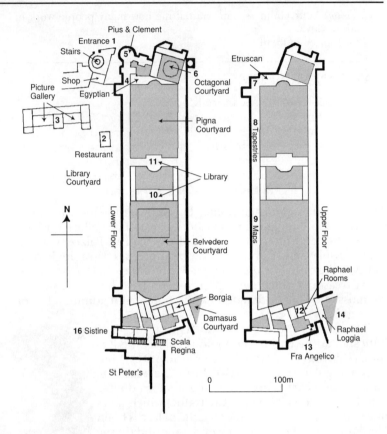

Plan of the Vatican Museum

from various papal collections, and the canvases from St Peter's basilica now replaced by mosaics. The gallery follows a chronological order from the Middle Ages down, and includes (among others) works by Giotto, Fra Angelico, Filippo Lippi, Pinturrichio, Perugino, Raphael (his last work, *The Transfiguration*, newly cleaned in 1980), da Vinci, Cranach, Caravaggio and Rubens.

Back inside the palace, the first rooms ahead house a small but valuable collection of **Egyptian Art** (4), and then the vast **Museum of Pius and Clement** (5), named after the 18th century popes who first put the papal collection of classical sculpture (the largest in the world) into some kind of order. Among the many fine objects, look for the Sala delle Muse which contains the 1st century BC *Belvedere Torso*, the inspiration of many Renaissance sculptors; and the octagonal courtyard (6) which displays the graceful 4th century BC *Apollo Belvedere*, and the tortured 1st century BC *Laocoon Group* discovered by Michelangelo in 1560 in the ruins of Nero's Golden House (see p.75). A priest and his sons, having warned their people that the Trojan Horse would destroy them, struggle with two gigantic snakes sent by Apollo to silence them. Their reconstructed arms, which for centuries gave the group an imbalance, have now been removed: you have to make up your own mind how the arms were originally meant to go.

On the floor above these rooms is a large display of **Etruscan Art** (7). From this, a 350m corridor leads to the other end of the palace, passing on the way a display of 16th century **Tapestries** (8) (now badly faded) made in Belgium from the Raphael cartoons now in London's Victoria and Albert Museum; and then of forty 16th century frescoed **Maps** (9) of the Italian provinces, which until 1870 formed part of the papal states. Halfway along this corridor, on both floors, is the *Biblioteca* or **Vatican Library** (10), with its priceless collection of books, codices and manuscripts going back to the 4th century AD. The collection includes the love letters written by Henry VIII to Anne Boleyn, and his petition for divorce from Catherine of Aragon. The brilliantly decorated main hall of the library, joining the two wings of the palace (11), was designed by Fontana, and displays the most interesting treasures in glass cases.

At the end of the long corridor are the *Stanze* or **Raphael Rooms** (12), which pope Julius III (having just commissioned Michelangelo to paint the Sistine ceiling) commissioned the young Raphael (aged 25) to decorate in 1508, to allow him to escape from the doom-laden Borgia Apartments downstairs (see below). His dining room is now known as the *Incendio* because it features an exciting fresco of the fire that threatened to destroy the area close to St Peter's in the 9th century. The library, known as the *Segnatura* because papal pardons were signed here, illustrates the harmony between Literature (the classical authors on *Mt Parnassus*), Science (philosophers and artists gathered in the *School of Athens*: Raphael has here included a self-portrait in the right corner), and the Christian Faith, where popes, bishops and theologians discuss (*Disputa*) the Blessed Sacrament. A third room of *Heliodorus* is named after the story of attempted sacrilege in 2 Maccabees 3, but is more famous for the frescoes of the *Mass of Bolsena*, where a doubting priest pierces an altar-bread which bleeds, and (over the window) the *Deliverance of Peter from Prison* with its brilliant interplay of light and dark. The last *Room of Constantine*, celebrating Constantine's crucial victory over his rival Maxentius at the Milvian Bridge in 312AD (in short, the victory of Christianity over paganism), is mainly the work of Raphael's pupil Giulio Romano.

In a tiny corner of the Raphael Rooms, and in sharp contrast to them, is the simple **Chapel of Nicholas V** (founder of the Vatican

Library) with graceful frescoes of the deacon saints Stephen and Lawrence painted by Fra Angelico in the 15th century (13). An adjoining corridor looking out onto the courtyard is known as **Raphael's Loggia** (14), and sometimes *Raphael's Bible*, since it is decorated throughout with scriptural scenes by the artist and his pupils. Having earlier been open to the weather, some are in a poor state of preservation, and tend to be closed to visitors.

Downstairs, the whole area beneath these Raphael rooms is occupied by the richly decorated family **Apartment of the Borgias** (15), commissioned by the unholy father Alexander VI, whose children, the lovely Lucrezia and the infamous Cesare, posed as models for Pinturrichio.

Signposts from here direct those interested to 55 rooms made available by pope Paul VI in the 1970's for his vast collection of **Modern Religious Art**. On display are works by Chirico, Corbusier, Dalí, Matisse, Modigliani, Munch, Rodin, Rouault, Sutherland and others.

The museum's last and most precious jewel comes as a fitting climax – the 15th century domestic chapel of pope Sixtus IV, known as the **Sistine Chapel** (16). The plain rectangular room, though already embellished by a richly decorated marble screen enclosing the sanctuary, was in need of decoration, and the greatest artists of the age – Botticelli, Ghirlandaio, Perugino and Pinturrichio – were engaged to put scenes from the life of Moses on the left wall of the chapel, and scenes from the life of Christ to match them on the right. This left the vast ceiling and the end wall above the altar, an area of over 1,000m². Michelangelo painted both, virtually single-handed. He produced what is universally acknowledged as a masterpiece unmatched by any other artist. Picasso said of it, 'no man, working with merely human power, could have painted this.' Napoleon showed what he thought of it by stabling his horses there.

The ceiling was his own idea. He was aged 34. He had been asked to paint portraits of the twelve apostles above the windows, and fill in the rest with decorative designs. Instead he got permission to use these twelve spaces for the five classic Sybils and seven Hebrew prophets who had looked forward to the redemption of the human race. Around these massive and moving figures, and above them, he turned the gently curved ceiling into a complex framework of twenty simulated pillars, capitals and plinths, surmounting each pillar with an exuberant naked youth, the very embodiment of the renaissance glorification of humanity. Finally, on the nine central panels (for which all the rest is an elaborate frame) he told the Genesis stories (beginning at the altar end) of the creation of the planets, of the earth, and of Adam and Eve; and then of their fall and of the deluge from which Noah was saved, only to drink himself into a stupor. In spite of the pessimistic ending, the story is uplifting rather than depressing. The task took him four and a half years, 1508-1512, most of the time bent double backwards. The central panels (and much of the rest of the ceiling) draw attention to the sublime dignity of the human race, sharing in the very beauty and goodness of God. The creation of Adam is overwhelmingly moving.

None of this optimism is apparent in the gigantic *Last Judgement* which Michelangelo was asked to paint on the wall behind the altar thirty years later, when he was aged 66. By that time Rome had been sacked by invaders only 13 years before, and Christendom had been split into two at the Reformation. In a gloomier mood, therefore, Michelangelo portrays Christ as a threatening Judge, hand raised as if ready to strike (Henry VIII had just rebelled against papal authority, 1533). On the left the dead are raised from the cloddish earth, and painfully hauled up to heaven by friends. On the right the damned are pushed down to the corner of the painting, where hell yawns to receive them. At the side of Christ, the gentle figure of Mary turns away, unable to bear the sight. The circular movement of the swirling figures makes one catch one's breath. Many were shocked when the fresco was first unveiled, not least by the nudity of the figures, and after Michelangelo's death loincloths were prudishly painted on top. Michelangelo himself impishly added a portrait of his chief critic, the papal master of ceremonies, assisting the demons in the bottom right hand corner. The man asked the pope to have the figure erased. The pope replied that he could intercede for those in purgatory, but had no jurisdiction in hell.

Both ceiling and wall underwent a thorough cleaning and restoration in the 1980's. The dirt of centuries needed to be removed, and a decision made about how much of the overpainting in the past was due to Michelangelo himself (to tone down colours that were too harsh?) and how much merely to contemporary taste (like the loincloths above). The controversy will no doubt continue, but there is equally no doubt that the newly restored chapel shines on today's visitors with a luminosity unknown to their predecessors, and they must make up their own minds.

The chapel plays an important role in the history, not only of art, but of the Church. It is here that the world's cardinals gather when a pope dies in order to elect his successor, the ballot papers being burnt in a stove to send a smoke signal to the outside world. Crowds gather here at all times in huge numbers, especially at high season, and the babel of a dozen guides competing in different languages is almost unavoidable. Those who wish to may leave the museum at this point straight into St Peter's square. Alternatively they may return to the entrance in order to enjoy the other treasures of this museum at greater leisure.

Michelangelo:
Honour and glory be to God, the Alpha and Omega, through whose help this work was begun and ended.
(Inscription on the figure of Jeremiah)

Thomas of Celano:
Day of wrath! O Day of mourning!
See fulfilled the prophets' warning!
Heav'n and earth in ashes burning!

O, what fear man's bosom rendeth
When from heaven the Judge descendeth,
On whose sentence all dependeth!

When the Judge his seat attaineth,
And each hidden deed arraigneth,
Nothing unavenged remaineth.

What shall I, frail man, be pleading,
Who for me be interceding,
When the just are mercy needing?

Righteous Judge of retribution,
Grant thy gift of absolution,
Ere that reckoning-days' conclusion.

With thy favoured sheep, O place me,
Nor among the goats abase me:
But to thy right hand upraise me.
(Dies Irae, trsl. W.J. Irons.)

VENERABILE (The English College)
see p.63.

VENEZIA, Piazza
see p.99.

VIA APPIA (Appian Way)
see p.32.

VIA DEL CORSO
see p.59.

VILLA BORGHESE

> Outside the Porta del Popolo, behind the Pincio.
> Metro A, Flaminio. Map CD3.

Originally named after the 17th century cardinal Scipione Borghese, this beautiful park has been public property since 1902. It has some fine walks, lakes, pavilions, monuments of historic figures (Victor Hugo, Byron, etc), and a zoo with free entrance for children and senior citizens. At its centre stands the **Piazza di Siena** where the International Horse Show takes place each May. At the east end of the park is the **Casino**, in which the connoisseur cardinal housed his outstanding collection of art, now called **Museo e Galleria Borghese**. It contains the world famous *David* (a self-portrait of Bernini when he was only 25), and Canova's *Pauline Bonaparte*, of which she excused the pose by explaining that it was very hot in the room. The exquisitely chosen paintings (by Botticelli, Caravaggio, Correggio, Cranach, Del Sarto, Domenichino, Pinturicchio, Raphael, Rubens, Titian, Van Dyck and Veronese) are second only to those in the Vatican galleries. The collection has been closed for some time for renovation works, but is hoped to open again in 1994. Open 9.00-13.00. Admission charge.

VILLA D'ESTE
see p.145.

VILLA MEDICI
see p.119.

WALLS OF ROME

Like many ancient cities, Rome is encircled by a wall, sharply distinguishing the buildings inside from the later housing developments outside. Because of its antiquity, Rome may claim to be the grandfather of all walled cities in the rest of Europe (Carcassonne, Rothenburg, Chester, Norwich, etc).

The earliest wall was erected by king Servius in the 5th century BC to enclose the hills on which ancient Rome was built. But a century later the city had already outgrown these walls, and when they were destroyed by an invasion of the Gauls, no attempts were made to replace them, and only a few traces of them remain.

A second and much larger wall was urgently built in the 3rd

century AD by the emperor Aurelian, when the Gothic invasions of the empire threatened Rome itself. These walls, 20km in length, with their impressive ramparts, towers, bastions and 16 massive gates, still survive, and are best seen in their southern portion between the gates of St Paul and St John, where parts are open to the public. They continue to mark off the 'essential Rome' from the inevitable more recent developments beyond. It is these walls which are shown in the outlines of Rome in this book.

EXCURSIONS

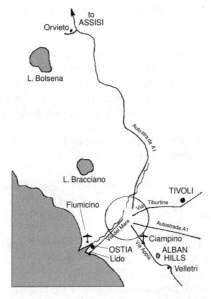

For those who wish to take time off from their sightseeing in Rome, a number of short excursions are available. Each of the first three listed below can be fitted into a half-day. Assisi will take a full and long day, and those who are able to stay overnight will find the extra time spent most rewarding.

ALBAN HILLS (Colli Albani)

Access by bus from the Metro A terminus
at Anagnina.

These charming hills lie 20-30km to the southeast of Rome, and offer some magnificent views and a welcome breath of fresh air. The hills rise to a height of 950m, and were formed by volcanic activity in the distant past. Two of the craters that remain now form the lakes of Albano and Nemi. Around these, emperors and wealthy Romans built their villas, and popes their castles. A circular tour of some of the *Castelli* towns may be made comfortably in a day, and will afford several opportunities of sampling their excellent wines.

Albano, the capital town of the district, was once the bishopric of Nicholas Breakspear, son of a priest, who became the only English pope, Adrian IV, in the 12th century.

Castel Gandolfo, on the rim of Lake Albano 120m below, is dominated by the pope's summer palace built in the 17th century. When he is on vacation from Rome, regular papal audiences are held here.

Lake Albano, one of the craters of the extinct volcano, is 2km wide and 170m deep, its excess water being drained off into the Tiber by a tunnel built in Roman times. The slopes to the northeast of the lake were the site of **Alba Longa**, capital of the Latin League which ruled this part of the world long before Rome was founded.

Marino, with its many churches, holds an annual autumn festival when the fountain in the main square runs with wine.

Grottaferrata, has an imposing abbey established here in the 11th century by Greek Catholic monks. Domenichino left some fine frescoes in the 17th century. There is a gift shop.

Frascati, justly famed for its wine, and perhaps the most attractive of the *Castelli*, has a cathedral with a memorial to the Young Pretender, son of James III, who died here in 1788. Above the town lies the ancient **Tusculum**, a favourite retreat of Cicero.

Rocca di Papa, clinging to the rim of another crater, the dried-out 'Camp of Hannibal', is the starting point for the ascent of **Monte**

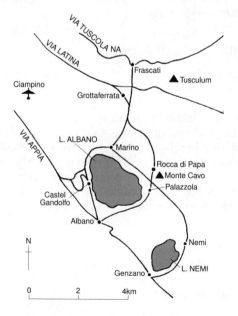

Cavo (1 hour). The conical hill was sacred to the Latin League, and was topped by a temple of Jupiter, later succeeded by a monastery built by Henry Stuart (Duke of York and Cardinal). The best views are from a little below the summit, which has in any case recently become a military area.

Palazzola, at the foot of Cavo and seemingly within shouting distance of Castel Gandolfo across the lake, is another monastery converted in 1920 into the summer villa of the English College in Rome (see p.63). It takes in guests all the year round in groups. Information from: Convento di Palazzola, Via dei Laghi km 10.8, Rocca di Papa, Prov. di Roma. Tel: 949 178.

Nemi, lies on a lake smaller than Albano, and is known for its delicious wild strawberries, and for the two Roman galleons dredged from the lake-bed in the 1930's. The retreating German army set fire to them in 1944.

Genzano, is famous for its celebration of *Corpus Christi*, when the street is carpeted with flowers.

OSTIA ANTICA

23km from Rome on the Via del Mare. By half-hourly train from Ostiense station (Metro B, Piramide) or by boat from Ponte Marconi (Metro B, S. Paolo). Open daily 9.00 to sunset. Admission charge, except for under 18's and over 60's. Restaurants. Winter visitors should be warned that the mosaics may be covered with sand for protection.

Ostia means 'Mouthtown'. It is where the Tiber once emptied into the sea, before centuries of neglect and tidal mud left it stranded 5km inland. Founded as early as the 4th century BC, it grew in importance under the Empire, when it was the base of the Imperial Fleet and Rome's principal harbour for the import of goods from abroad. This is where St Augustine's mother Monica came to catch a boat back to her native Algeria, but fell ill, died and was buried in 387AD. With the subsequent decay of Rome, there was no future for Ostia, and it too was buried in the sands of time.

The happy outcome is that, since Mussolini's draining of the whole area in the 1930's, it has been possible for archæologists to disinter the town, uncluttered by any later renaissance or baroque additions, and to reveal more clearly than any place in Rome the everyday life of classical times. Walls, gates, streets, dwellings, shops, baths, theatres, temples, warehouses, markets, gardens – all are open to view, in the perfumed setting of cypresses, pines and wild herbs. The mosaics are a sheer delight, especially those which display the trade of the occupant in the business district. The small museum near the river is well worth a visit for its display of finds from the site. Travellers with a long wait at Fiumicino airport are offered free travel to the site (daily at 11.00, 13.00 and 15.00).

Those looking for a day at the seaside (**Lido di Ostia**, 5km further on) should be warned that the whole of the beach has been divided up into private bathing establishments, for which another admission charge is made.

St Augustine:

As the day approached when she was to die ... we stood alone at a window looking out onto a garden in Ostia, where we were resting after a long journey and preparing ourselves for the sea voyage [back to Africa]. We had a long and a most sweet conversation ... At the end of it she said, 'As far as I am concerned, my son, I have no further desire to live on. I can't imagine what I still need to do here, or why. My hopes in this world are at an end. There was one thing I still wanted to live for – to see you become a catholic Christian before I died. This God has graciously granted me. What more can I wish for here?' ...

She eventually sank into a fever. When she came out of it and saw me and my brother, she asked, 'Where was I?' Then she looked at us in our grief and said, 'You must bury your mother here.' I stayed silent, holding back my tears. My brother said something about her surely wanting to die to home, and not abroad. She looked at him anxiously, her eyes reproving him for such a worldly thought, and then turned to me and said, 'Look what he is saying!' Then she said to both of us, 'Bury me where you like, it doesn't matter. Only this matters, that wherever you are you remember me at the altar of the Lord'.

She had always been most careful about the arrangements for being buried next to her husband, and hoped that after her long journey overseas it would be granted to her to have the same earth covering them both. I don't know when she gave up this idea ... but I learned afterwards that when friends who were with us at Ostia asked whether she was not afraid of leaving her body so far away from Rome, she replied, 'Nothing is far away from God. Do you imagine that at the end of the world he won't know the place from which to raise me from the dead?'

In the ninth day of her sickness, and in her 56th year and my 33rd, that holy soul was released from its body. I closed my eyes, my heart filled with an overwhelming grief, and the tears came.

(Confessions IX, 10-12)

TIVOLI

31km east of Rome on the Via Tiburtina (SS5).
Easy access (1 hour) by ACOTRAL coaches from
the Metro B terminus, Rebibbia.

This delightful hilltown, known to the ancients as *Tibur*, was a
favourite summer resort of the Roman aristocracy. It has become
best known for its **Villa d'Este**, built on the edge of town by the 16th
century cardinal d'Este, son of Lucrezia Borgia, who was determined to outshine all the renaissance gardens of his predecessors,
and succeeded. The rather foreboding house through which one
enters (once a monastery) leads onto a balcony. Below, in terrace
beneath terrace, lies the garden of one's dreams, shaded by the
tallest cypresses anywhere in Italy, and alive with the sound of a
hundred fountains, spouting, gushing, splashing, cascading, gur-
gling, trilling, or just gently flowing from basin to basin, and from
sculpture to sculpture, as the deviated river Anio makes its way
down the steep slope on which the fantasy garden has been built.
In its heyday, the gardens included a number of aquatic jokes,
designed at the press of a button to drench unsuspecting guests.
Neglected for years, they were nationalised in 1918, and restored
to something of their former glory. Beauty, as everyone knows, is
in the eye of the beholder. In 1749 the poet Thomas Gray dismissed
the whole thing as 'Half the Tiber pissing into two thousand
chamber pots.' Yet a century later the composer Liszt was inspired
here to compose his *Fountains of the Villa d'Este*. Open 9.00 to one
hour before sunset. *Son et Lumière* in summer. Fountains tend to be
switched off in the lunch hour. Closed Mondays. Admission charge,
except for the under 18's and over 60's.

Those who have the time may wish to go back into town to see
pope Gregory XII's attempt in 1835 to compete with the flamboy-
ant cardinal in his **Villa Gregoriana** (admission charge). Just
beyond is the **Great Waterfall** (**Grande Cascate**), no longer as
impressive as of old because of hydro-electric requirements.

Approximately 5km south of the town (the ACOTRAL coach
will drop you there in its way into Tivoli) are the impressive remains
of **Hadrian's Villa** (**Villa Adriana**), the largest of ancient times. It
covers 170 acres, and is only worth visiting by those who have at
least two hours to spare. It is to this pleasant hillside that the 2nd
century emperor Hadrian, exhausted by his building activities
across his vast empire, from the frozen north (Hadrian's Wall) to
the torrid east (Jerusalem's *Aelia Capitolina*) came to retire. But he
continued building even here, and set up not only a 'stately
pleasure dome', but a kind of 18th century 'folly' to reproduce in
miniature the many wonders he had seen on his imperial tours. The
visit includes a Greek theatre, an island retreat, two sets of Roman

baths, a stadium, a library and a palace. The coffee shop at the entrance provides a scale model to help the visitor. All the classical statuary has flown, since Renaissance times, to museums in the countries Hadrian once ruled. But visitors come not to reconstruct the stones, simply to revel in their incomparable setting. Opening times as at Villa d'Este. Admission charge, except for under 18's and over 60's.

ASSISI

183km from Rome. Easiest access is by coach (3 hours). By train, change at Orte and Foligno. The station is 3km from the town: regular buses.

An excursion to Assisi, even if only for the day, provides a salutary break from sightseeing in Rome, and a perfect contrast. Here is mediæval Italy at its most picturesque and unspoilt, and even the vast numbers of pilgrims who have flocked here, year after year for eight centuries, do not mar its charm.

Born in 1182, Francesco Bernadone was the son of a rich merchant, then on a business trip to France – hence the name. Francis led a wild and frivolous youth. It was only when he was taken prisoner in a war with nearby Perugia that he was brought to his senses. He returned determined to renounce his privileged background, and even stripped off his clothes publicly to return them to his father. He would live a life of utter poverty, and devote his life to the service of those in need, his one inspiration the gospel Jesus. Dozens of his contemporaries joined him, and they were able to convince the pope (who had just dreamed of his tottering Lateran church saved from collapse by a beggar, see p.81), that this kind of witness could restore some credibility to the corrupt Christianity of the time. With papal approval the movement spread like fire throughout Italy, until those who attended the annual 'chapter' of review held in Assisi numbered thousands. Against Francis' will, the movement was codified into a formal religious 'order'. Francis himself, by then blind, retired to live as a hermit, and died at the age of 44. Within two years he was acclaimed as a saint, and chosen (along with Catherine of Siena) as patron of Italy.

The church of **St Mary of the Angels** stands in the valley, near the railway station. It provides a fitting introduction to the story of the 'Franciscans', who first used the field or 'portion' (*Porziuncula*) donated to them by the local Benedictines as the headquarters for their work. The simple chapel they used has been frescoed inside and out, and stands dwarfed by the grandiose church built around it by Vignola in the 17th century. The cell used by Francis and in which he died is still to be seen behind the chapel, and the left transept has a fine della Robbia statue of him in glazed enamel. The sacristy leads to a garden whose roses have remained thornless, it is claimed, ever since Francis rolled about in them as a penance. What is an undisputed fact is that the doves (whom in his days Francis insisted on freeing from their cages) have made a permanent nest in the hands of his statue here.

There is a small museum (Cimabue, Pisano, Tiberio di Assisi) with a gift shop.

D. Lundy:
Sing of a girl that the angels surround,
dust in her hand, and straw in her hair.
Kings and their crowns will fall to the ground
before the child that mother will bear.

Noticias Aliadas:
Mary the slum-dweller
Mary who longed for the liberation of her people
Mary who sang to God of the poor
Mary homeless in Bethlehem
Mother of the longed-for Saviour
Mary exiled from her native land
Mary pilgrim with her people
Blessed are you among women.

Assisi (see plan, p.148) itself lies on the hill to the north, 3km ahead up a winding road. The fortress of the 12th century **Rocca Maggiore** dominates the mediæval walled town, but its most striking feature is the massive church and monastery of **St Francis** jutting out from the eastern brow of the hill, like some baronial castle – the very antithesis, one would have thought, of what the *poverello* Francis himself had stood for. But his devotees insisted, within two years of his death, that no tribute less grandiose would do, and finished it two years later.

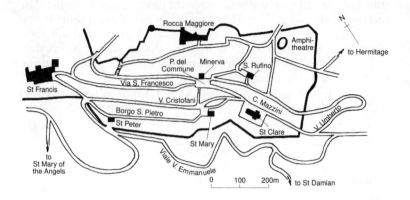

Plan of Assisi

The **Lower Church**, in Romanesque style, is a treasure house of frescoes by the masters of the early Renaissance: Cimabue, Giotto, Simone Martini and Lorenzetti. The lighting is poor, and coins will be useful for illuminating individual items. Above the high altar, there are Giotto (?) frescoes of Francis' 'marriage' to his three vows of Poverty, Chastity and Obedience. Stairs lead down to the **Crypt**, constructed as recently as 1818 to house a gold-lined tomb for Francis' body, hidden till then for safe-keeping.

The **Upper Church** needs no illumination. Its lofty gothic construction, the first of its kind in Italy, fills it with light. Here too Cimabue has contributed (the crucifixion), as also Cavallini (upper walls), but the main feature is the life of Francis, done in 28 scenes round the lower walls by pupils of Giotto, fading somewhat after so many centuries, but untouched by restorers. There is a gift shop.

The main road back uphill into town leads shortly (700m) to the **Town Centre** (**Piazza del Commune**), the site of the old Roman Forum (the original stones may be seen in the **Civic Museum**). Here stands proudly the original façade of the 2,000 year old **Temple of Minerva**, whose interior (like Rome's Minerva, see p.92) became a baroque church in the 16th century. Goethe cynically asked, 'Whose was the desecration?' Steps down from the piazza lead to a signposted stable in which Francis is said to have been born in a cattle-crib (*presepio*) – a dramatic expression of the conviction that his life was like that of Jesus. Steps up from the piazza lead to the stern 12th century **Cathedral of S. Rufino**, in whose font were baptised not only Francis and Clare, but also the grandson of Barbarossa, who was to become the Holy Roman Emperor Frederick II, and who had more than his share of squabbles with popes. From here an easy path goes up to the town's highpoint, the **Rocca**

Maggiore. Further east, still inside the walls, are the remains of a Roman amphitheatre.

300m further along the main road from the town centre is the Piazza S. Chiara, with its noble rose-tinted church of **St Clare**. Its western rose window is a sheer joy in stone outside, and in coloured light within. Here is displayed the body of the saint, though its leathery appearance may not appeal to all as evidence of incorruption. More eloquent is the famous 12th century late Byzantine cross in a side chapel which is said to have spoken to Francis, commanding him to rebuilt the crumbling church. It still speaks to many today.

The crumbling church of **St Damian** which, ever practical, Francis tackled as the first of his tasks, lies 2km downhill from St Clare's. An oasis of calm away from the town's bustle, many pilgrims find that this simple monastery sums up better than anything else in Assisi the spirit of St Francis. It was here that in 1212 he settled the noblewoman Clare who wished to follow his lifestyle, and the first 'Poor Clares' who wanted to join her. It was in the peaceful cloister here, when he was close to death, that he composed the *Canticle of the Sun*, which still inspires those who read it to see, as Francis did, the relatedness of all God's creatures (see below). The refectory has been left as it was in Clare's days, with a vase of flowers marking her place. The little church, frescoed throughout by pupils of Perugino, has its wooden choir stalls inscribed with the moving words: NON. VOX. SED. VOTUM. NON. CLAMOR. SED. AMOR. NON. CORDULA. SED. COR. PSALLIST. IN. AURE. DEI. LINGUA. CONSONET. MENTI. ET. MENS. CONCORDET. DEO. 1504, which could be translated as:

> It is not the voice but the choice,
> Not the clarity but the charity,
> Not the harp but the heart,
> That makes music in the ear of God,
> Let your tongue reflect your thoughts,
> And your thoughts be in tune with God. (1994)

Further up the hill behind Assisi, 750m above the plain, and reachable only on foot or by taxi (10 minutes), is the **Hermitage (Eremo delle Carceri)** where the early Franciscans spent times of penance in caves. It was here that Francis underwent the mystical experience which left on his feet and hands and side the marks or *stigmata* of the crucified Christ. The situation, in a wooded ravine, is breathtaking. The buildings were erected by the great Franciscan preacher St Bernadine in the 15th century.

No-one leaves Assisi unaffected. Whether it is the feeling that one has stepped back into mediæval Europe, the genuine courtesy and friendliness of the local people, the challenge of Francis' insistence on simply returning to gospel values, or his vision of the

149

one-ness of all creation where both the moon and the Muslim, birds and Buddhists, are our sisters and brothers – Assisi is a place to which, even without a Trevi fountain, one hopes one day to return. It is no chance that pope John Paul II, in making a worldwide appeal for peace, has successfully invited all the religious leaders of the world to meet here at the feet of St Francis.

Those visiting in Holy Week can take part in torchlight processions. St Clare's victory over the Saracen attacks on the town is celebrated on 21st June. In July and August there is a musical festival. Over the first weekend of October, the feast of St Francis, bands from all over the Italian provinces compete, with much marching and acrobatic flag-throwing.

St Francis:
Laudato sii, o mi Signore (May you be praised, my Lord)

Yes, be praised in all your creatures,
Brother Sun and Sister Moon,
In the stars and in the wind,
Air and fire and flowing water. Laudato sii …

For our sister, Mother Earth,
She who feeds us and sustains us,
For her fruits, her grass, her flowers,
For the mountains and the oceans. Laudato sii …

Praise for those who spread forgiveness,
Those who share your peace with others,
Bearing trials and sickness bravely:
Even Sister Death won't harm them. Laudato sii …

Praise to you, Father most holy,
Praise and thanks to you, Lord Jesus,
Praise to you, most holy Spirit,
Life and joy of all creation. Laudato sii …
(*Canticle of the Sun, trsl. Damian Lundy*)

Contemporary Prayers:
Give us, Lord God,
a vision of our world as your love would make it:
a world where the weak are protected,
and none go hungry or poor;
a world where the benefits of civilised life
are shared, and everyone can enjoy them;
a world where different races, nations and cultures
live in tolerance and mutual respect;
a world where peace is built with justice,
and justice is guided by love.
And give us the inspiration and courage to build it
through Jesus Christ our Lord. Amen.

Spirit of God, powerful and unpredictable as the wind,
you came upon the followers of Jesus on the first Whit Sunday
and swept them off their feet,
so that they found themselves doing
what they thought they never had it in them to do.
It is you who through the ages
have fired people with enthusiasm
to go about telling the good news of Jesus
and serving other people for his sake.
Spirit of God, powerful and unpredictable as the wind,
come upon us as we pray
and become the driving force of our lives.

(SCM 1967)

St Francis' advice to his friars:
Go and preach the gospel.
Use words if necessary.

RESOURCE MATERIAL FOR WORSHIP

The liturgical material which follows has been taken from four sources: the Roman Catholic *Missal* (RC); The Church of England *Alternative Services Book* (CE); Caryl Micklem's *Contemporary Prayers* (CM); and Huub Oosterhuis' *Ten Table Prayers* (HO). No complete text of any one service is offered. Instead, enough material is provided for Christians of any tradition to use as they see fit in their own customary pattern of Communion, Eucharist, Mass or Lord's Supper.

1. INTRODUCTION

a. (RC) The grace and peace of God our Father
and the Lord Jesus Christ be with you.
And also with you.

2. OPENING PRAYERS

a. (CE) **Almighty God,**
to whom all hearts are open,
all desires known,
and from whom no secrets are hidden:
cleanse the thoughts of our hearts
by the inspiration of your Holy Spirit,
that we may perfectly love you,
and worthily magnify your holy Name;
through Christ our Lord. Amen.

b. (CM) Jesus said:
I did not come to come to invite virtuous people,
but sinners.
Merciful God, we do not dare come to this table
trusting in our own goodness and virtue.
We come because we are sinful and need forgiveness.
We come because we are hungry for life and need to
be fed.
We come because Christ has invited us sinners.
We come in gratitude and wonder
to offer our very selves to you
in worship and adoration.
Father, accept our praise,
through Jesus Christ our Lord.

3. PRAYERS OF PENITENCE

a. (RC)   You were sent to heal the contrite: Lord, have mercy.
          Lord, have mercy.
          You came to call sinners: Christ, have mercy.
          Christ, have mercy.
          You plead for us at the right hand of the Father:
             Lord, have mercy
          Lord, have mercy.
          May almighty God have mercy on us,
          forgive us our sins,
          and bring us to everlasting life.
          Amen.

b. (CE)   **Almighty God, our heavenly Father,**
          we have sinned against you and against our
          **   fellow men,**
          in thought and word and deed,
          through negligence, through weakness,
          through our own deliberate fault.
          We are truly sorry,
          and repent of all our sins.

          For the sake of your Son Jesus Christ, who died
          **   for us,**
          forgive us all that is past;
          and grant that we may serve you in newness of life
          to the glory of your name. Amen.

c. (CM)   Lord our God,
          great, eternal, wonderful, utterly to be trusted:
          you give life to us all,
          you help those who come to you,
          you give hope to those who appeal to you.
          Forgive our sins, secret and open,
          and rid us of every habit of thought foreign to
             the gospel.
          Set our hearts and consciences at peace,
          so that we may bring our prayers to you without fear;
          through Jesus Christ our Lord.

4. ASSURANCE OF PARDON

a. (CE)   Almighty God,
          who forgives all who truly repent,
          have mercy upon you,
          pardon and deliver you from all your sins,

confirm and strengthen you in all goodness,
and keep you in life eternal;
through Jesus Christ our Lord. **Amen.**

b. (CM) Here are words you may trust,
words that merit full acceptance:
Christ Jesus came into the world to save sinners.
Now to the King of all worlds,
immortal, invisible, the only wise God.
be honour and glory for ever and ever. **Amen.**

5. GLORIA IN EXCELSIS

**Glory to God in the highest,
and peace to his people on earth.**

**Lord God, heavenly King,
almighty God and Father,
we worship you, we give you thanks,
we praise you for your glory.**

**Lord Jesus Christ, only Son of the Father,
Lord God, Lamb of God,
you take away the sin of the world:
have mercy on us;
you are seated at the right hand of the Father:
receive our prayer;
for you alone are the Holy One,
you alone are the Lord,
you alone are the Most High, Jesus Christ.**

**With the Holy Spirit,
in the glory of God the Father. Amen.**

6. SCRIPTURE READINGS

7. THE CREED

**I believe in God the Father Almighty,
Creator of heaven and earth;
and in Jesus Christ his only Son our Lord,
who was conceived by the Holy Ghost,
born of the Virgin Mary;
suffered under Pontius Pilate,
was crucified, dead, and buried;**

he descended into hell;
the third day he rose again from the dead;
he ascended into heaven,
sitteth at the right hand of God the Father Almighty;
from thence he shall come to judge the living and
the dead.
I believe in the Holy Ghost;
the holy Catholic Church;
the communion of saints;
the forgiveness of sins;
the resurrection of the body,
and life everlasting. Amen.

8.   INTERCESSIONS

a. (CE)   Let us pray for the Church and for the world;
and let us thank God for his goodness.
Almighty God, our heavenly Father,
who promised through your Son Jesus Christ
to hear us when we pray in faith:
we pray for ...
Strengthen your Church
to carry forward the work of Christ;
that we and all who confess your Name
may unite in your truth,
live together in your love,
and reveal your glory to the world.
Lord, in your mercy
Hear our prayer.

We pray for the nations of the world ...
Give wisdom to all in authority;
direct all nations in the ways of justice and
of peace;
that men may honour one another,
and seek the common good.
Lord in your mercy
Hear our prayer.

We pray for our friends ...
Give grace to us, our families and friends,
and to all neighbours in Christ;
that we may serve him in one another,
and love as he loves us.
Lord, in your mercy
Hear our prayer.

We pray for the sick and the suffering ...
those who mourn ...
those without faith ...
we pray for all who serve and relieve them ...
Comfort and heal all those
who suffer in body, mind, or spirit;
give them courage and hope in their troubles;
and bring them the joy of your salvation.
Lord, in your mercy
Hear our prayer.

We commemorate the departed ...
We commend all men to your unfailing love,
that in them your will may be fulfilled;
and we rejoice at the faithful witness   ·
of your saints in every age,
praying that we may share with them
in your eternal kingdom.
Lord, in your mercy
**Accept these prayers for the sake of your Son,
our Saviour Jesus Christ. Amen.**

b. (CM)   Lord God,
the story of your love for us
makes us realise that there are many others,
as well as ourselves,
who need your help and your grace.
So we bring our prayers to you:
for those who suffer pain;
for those whose minds are disturbed
or have never matured;
for those who have not had the opportunity
to realise their potential;
for those who are satisfied with something less
than the life for which they were made;
for those who know their guilt,
their shallowness, their need,
but who do not know Jesus;
for those who know that they must shortly die;
for those who cannot wait to die.

Lord God,
your Son has taken all our sufferings upon himself
and has transformed them.
Help us, who offer these prayers,

to take the sufferings of others upon ourselves,
and so, by your grace,
become the agents of your transforming love.

9. EUCHARISTIC PRAYER

a. (RC) The Lord be with you
And also with you.
Lift up your hearts.
We lift them up to the Lord.
Let us give thanks to the Lord our God.
It is right to give him thanks and praise.

Father,
it is our duty and our salvation,
always and everywhere
to give you thanks
through your beloved Son, Jesus Christ.
He is the Word through whom you made the universe,
the Saviour you sent to redeem us.
By the power of the Holy Spirit
he took flesh and was born of the Virgin Mary.
For our sake he opened his arms on the cross;
he put an end to death
and revealed the resurrection.
In this he fulfilled your will
and won for you a holy people.
And so we join the angels and saints
in proclaiming your glory:
Holy, holy, holy Lord, God of power and might,
Heaven and earth are full of your glory.
Hosanna in the highest.
Blessed is he who comes in the name of the Lord.
Hosanna in the highest.

(Roman Canon)
We come to your, Father,
with praise and thanksgiving,
through Jesus Christ your Son.
Through him we ask you to accept and bless
these gifts we offer you in sacrifice.
We offer them for your holy catholic Church:
watch over it, Lord, and guide it;
grant it peace and unity throughout the world.
We offer them for N. our pope,
for N. our bishop,

and for all who hold and teach the catholic faith
that comes to us from the apostles.

Remember, Lord, your people,
especially those for whom we now pray, N. and N.
Remember all of us gathered here before you.
You know how firmly we believe in you
and dedicate ourselves to you.

We offer you this sacrifice of praise
for ourselves and those who are dear to us.
We pray to you, our living and true God,
for our well-being and redemption.

In union with the whole Church
we honour Mary
the ever-virgin mother of Jesus Christ our Lord
    and God.
We honour Joseph, her husband,
the apostles and martyrs,
Peter and Paul,
Andrew, James, John, Thomas, James, Philip,
Bartholomew, Matthew, Simon and Jude;
We honour Linus, Cletus, Clement, Sixtus,
Cornelius, Cyprian, Lawrence, Chrysogonus,
John and Paul, Cosmas and Damian,
and all the saints.
May their merits and prayers
gains us your constant help and protection.

Father, accept this offering
from your whole family.
Grant us your peace in this life,
save us from final damnation,
and count us among those you have chosen.
Bless and approve our offering;
make it acceptable to you,
an offering in spirit and in truth.
Let it become for us
the body and blood of Jesus Christ,
your only Son, our Lord.

The day before he suffered
he took bread in his sacred hands,
and looking up to heaven

to you, his almighty Father,
he gave you thanks and praise.
He broke the bread,
gave it to his disciples, and said:
Take this, all of you, and eat it:
this is my body which will be given up
    for you.

When supper was ended, he took the cup.
Again he gave you thanks and praise,
gave the cup to his disciples, and said:
Take this, all of you, and drink from it:
this is the cup of my blood,
the blood of the new and everlasting
    covenant.
It will be shed for you and for all
so that sins may be forgiven.
Do this in memory of me.

Let us proclaim the mystery of faith:

1.   **Christ has died,**
     Christ is risen,
     Christ will come again.

2.   **Dying you destroyed our death,**
     rising you restored our life.
     Lord Jesus, come in glory.

3.   **When we eat this bread and drink this cup,**
     we proclaim your death, Lord Jesus,
     until you come in glory.

4.   **Lord, by your cross and resurrection**
     you have set us free.
     You are the Saviour of the world.

Father, we celebrate the memory of Christ,
    your Son.
We, your people and your ministers,
recall his passion,
his resurrection from the dead,
and his ascension into glory;
and from the many gifts you have given us
we offer to you, God of glory and majesty,

this holy and perfect sacrifice:
the bread of life
and the cup of eternal salvation.
Look with favour on these offerings
and accept them as once you accepted
the gifts of your servant Abel,
the sacrifice of Abraham, our father in faith,
and the bread and wine offered by your priest
    Melchisedech.

Almighty God,
we pray that your angel may take this sacrifice
to your altar in heaven.
Then, as we receive from this altar
the sacred body and blood of your Son,
let us be filled with every grace and blessing.
Remember, Lord, those who have died
and have gone before us marked with the sign of faith,
especially those for whom we now pray, N. and N.
May these, and all who sleep in Christ,
find in your presence
light, happiness and peace.

For ourselves, too, we ask
some share in the fellowship of your apostles
    and martyrs,
with John the Baptist, Stephen, Matthias, Barnabas,
Ignatius, Alexander, Marcellinus, Peter,
Felicity, Perpetua, Agatha, Lucy,
Agnes, Cecilia, Anastasia
and all the saints.
Though we are sinners,
we trust in your mercy and love.
Do not consider what we truly deserve,
but grant us your forgiveness.

Through Christ our Lord
you give us all these gifts.
You fill them with life and goodness,
you bless them and make them holy.

Through him, with him, in him,
in the unity of the Holy Spirit,
all glory and honour is yours,
almighty Father,
for ever and ever.
Amen.

b. (CE)   The Lord be with you *or* The Lord is here.
                And also with you.   **His Spirit is with us.**
                Lift up your hearts.
                We lift them to the Lord.
                Let us give thanks to the Lord our God.
                It is right to give him thanks and praise.

It is indeed right,
it is our duty and our joy,
at all times and in all places
to give you thanks and praise,
holy Father, heavenly King,
almighty and eternal God,
through Jesus Christ your only Son our Lord.

For he is your living Word;
through him you have created all things from
     the beginning,
and formed us in your own image.

Through him you have freed us from the slavery
     of sin,
giving him to be born as man and to die upon
     the cross;
you raised him from the dead
and exalted him to your right hand on high.

Through him you have sent upon us
your holy and lifegiving Spirit,
and made us a people for your own possession.

Therefore with angels and archangels,
and with all the company of heaven,
we proclaim your great and glorious name,
for ever praising you and saying:

Holy, holy, holy Lord,
God of power and might,
heaven and earth are full of your glory.
Hosanna in the highest.
Blessed is he who comes in the name of the Lord.
Hosanna in the highest.

Accept our praises, heavenly Father,
through your Son our Saviour Jesus Christ;
and as we follow his example and obey his command,

161

grant that by the power of your Holy Spirit
these gifts of bread and wine
may be to us his body and his blood.

Who in the same night that he was betrayed,
took bread and gave you thanks;
he broke it and gave it to his disciples, saying:
Take, eat; this is my body which is given for you;
do this in remembrance of me.
In the same way, after supper,
he took the cup and gave you thanks;
he gave it to them, saying:
Drink this, all of you;
this is my blood of the new covenant,
which is shed for you and for many
    for the forgiveness of sins.
Do this, as often as you drink it,
in remembrance of me.

Christ has died:
Christ is risen:
Christ will come again.

Therefore, heavenly Father,
we remember his offering of himself
made once for all upon the cross,
and proclaim his mighty resurrection and glorious
    ascension.
As we look for his coming in glory,
we celebrate with this bread and this cup
his one perfect sacrifice.

Accept through him, our great high priest,
this our sacrifice of thanks and praise;
and as we eat and drink these holy gifts
in the presence of your divine majesty,
renew us by your Spirit,
inspire us with your love,
and unite us in the body of your Son,
Jesus Christ our Lord.

Through him, and with him, and in him,
by the power of the Holy spirit,
with all who stand before you in earth and heaven,
we worship you, Father almighty,
in songs of everlasting praise:

**Blessing and honour and glory and power
be yours for ever and ever. Amen.**

c. (HO)   The Lord be with you.
              The Lord will preserve you.
              Lift up your hearts.
              Our hearts are with the Lord;
              Let us thank the Lord our God.
              He is worthy of our gratitude.

We thank you
for you are a God of people,
for we may call you our God and our Father,
for you hold our future in your hands,
for this world touches your heart.

You called us and broke through our deafness,
you appeared in our darkness,
you opened our eyes with your light,
you ordered everything for the best for us
and brought us to life.

Blessed are you, the source of all that exists.
We thirst for you,
because you have made us thirsty.
Our hearts are restless
until we are secure in you,
with Jesus Christ our Lord.

With all who have gone before us in faith,
we praise your name, O Lord our God.
You are our hope
and we thank you, full of joy,
adoring you with the words:

**Holy, holy, holy,
Lord of all powers.
Heaven and earth
are full of your glory.
Come and deliver us,
Lord most high.
Blessed is he who comes
in the name of the Lord.
Come and deliver us,
Lord most high.**

163

We thank you
for the sake of your beloved Son,
whom you called and sent
to serve us and to give us light,
to bring your kingdom
to the poor,
to bring redemption
to all captive people,
and to be forever
and for all mankind
the likeness and the form
of your constant love and goodness.

We thank you
for this unforgettable man
who has fulfilled everything
that is human –
our life and death.
We thank you
because he gave himself,
heart and soul, to this world.

For, on the night that he was delivered up,
he took bread into his hands
and raising his eyes to you,
God, his almighty Father,
he gave thanks
and broke the bread
and gave it to his friends
with the words:
Take and eat,
this is my body for you.
Do this in memory of me.

He also took the cup
and, giving thanks to you, said:
This cup is the new covenant in my blood
shed for you and for all mankind
so that sins may be forgiven.
Every time you drink this cup,
you will do it in memory of me.

So whenever we eat of this bread
and drink from this cup
we proclaim the death of the Lord
until he comes.

Therefore, Lord our God,
we present this sign of our faith
and therefore we call to mind
the suffering and death of your Son,
his resurrection from the dead,
his entry into your glory,
recalling that he
who is exalted at your right hand
will intercede for us
and that he will come
to do justice to the living and the dead
on the day that you have appointed.

Send us your Spirit
who is life, justice and light.
O God,
you want the well-being of all men,
not their unhappiness
and not death.
Take all violence away from us.
Curb the passion
that makes us seek each other's lives.
Give us peace on earth
by the power of Jesus Christ,
your Son here among us.
We ask and implore you
to grant us this.

Then your name will be made holy,
through him and with him and in him,
everywhere on earth and here and now,
and for ever and ever.
Amen.

10. COMMUNION

We break this bread
to share in the body of Christ.
**Though we are many, we are one body,
because we all share in one bread.**

**Lamb of God, you take away the sins of the world:
have mercy on us.
Lamb of God, you take away the sins of the world:
have mercy on us.
Lamb of God, you take away the sins of the world:
grant us peace.**

or: **Jesus, Lamb of God: have mercy on us.**
Jesus, bearer of our sins: have mercy on us
Jesus, redeemer of the world: give us your peace.

Draw near with faith.
Receive the body of our Lord Jesus Christ which he
    gave for you,
and his blood which he shed for you.
Eat and drink in remembrance that he died for you,
and feed on him in your hearts by faith with
    thanksgiving.

11. CONCLUDING PRAYERS

a. (CM) Holy Father,
we thank you for making your home among us
and revealing to us
the knowledge, faith and indestructible life
that come through Jesus, your Son.
Deliver your Church from every evil
and teach it to love you perfectly.
As bread like this was once scattered over the fields
and gathered together to become one,
so gather your people from the four winds into one
    Church.
To you be glory for ever.

b. (CE) Father of all, we give you thanks and praise,
that when we were still far off
you met us in your Son and brought us home.
Dying and living, he declared your love,
gave us grace, and opened the gate of glory.
May we who share Christ's body live his risen life;
we who drink his cup bring life to others;
we whom the Spirit lights give light to the world.
Keep us firm in the hope you have set before us,
so we and all your children shall be free,
and the whole earth live to praise your name;
through Christ our Lord.
Amen.

Almighty God,
we thank you for feeding us
with the body and blood of your Son Jesus Christ.
Through him we offer you our souls and bodies
to be a living sacrifice.

Send us out in the power of your Spirit
to live and work to your praise and glory. Amen.

12. BLESSING

a. (CE) The peace of God, which passes all understanding,
keep your hearts and minds
in the knowledge and love of God,
and of his Son Jesus Christ our Lord;
and the blessing of God almighty,
the Father, the Son, and the Holy Spirit,
be among you, and remain with you always.
Amen.

Go in peace to love and serve the Lord.
In the name of Christ. Amen.

or: Go in the peace of Christ.
Thanks be to God.

b. (RC) The Lord be with you.
And also with you.

May almighty God bless you,
the Father, and the Son, and the Holy Spirit.
Amen.

Go, in the peace of Christ.
or: The Mass is ended, go in peace.
or: Go in peace to love and serve the Lord.
Thanks be to God.

DEVOTIONS

LENT STATIONS

The old Roman Missal prefaced the special Mass for each day of Lent with the words 'Station at St. X' (one of the churches in Rome). It referred to the long-standing Roman custom of celebrating the forty days of Lent as a community, with the bishop of Rome meeting his people at a different church each day for Mass. The devotion is still alive today, giving even the most obscure churches an opportunity to greet all comers with strewn bay leaves, and to display all their treasures.

Some Station churches are very popular, and crowds always flock to the Ash Wednesday service when the pope launches Lent at S. Sabina (see p.123). Because of restoration work and other reasons, the old Missal headings are not always strictly adhered to. Those who are in Rome for Lent and wish to attend the services should consult the notice outside the previous day's Station church.

The devotions consist of the celebration of Mass in the morning, and a solemn procession in the evening, during which the Litany of the Saints is sung.

LITANY OF THE SAINTS

Kyrie, eleison	Lord, have mercy
Christe, eleison	Christ, have mercy
Kyrie, eleison	Lord, have mercy
Christe, audi nos	Christ, hear us
Christe, exaudi nos.	Christ, graciously hear us.
Pater de coelis, Deus, miserere nobis	God, the Father in heaven, have mercy on us
Fili Redemptor mundi, Deus, miserere nobis	Son of God, Redeemer of the world, have mercy on us
Spiritus Sancte, Deus, miserere nobis	Holy Spirit of God, have mercy on us

Sancta Trinitas, unus Deus, miserere nobis.	Holy Trinity, one God, have mercy on us.
Sancta Maria, ora pro nobis	Holy Mary, pray for us
Sancta Dei Genetrix, ora pro nobis	Holy Mother of God, pray for us
Sancta Virgo virginum, ora pro nobis	Holiest of all virgins pray for us
Sancte Michael, ora ...	St Michael, pray ...
Sancte Gabriel, ora ...	St Gabriel, pray ...
Sancte Raphael, ora ...	St Raphael, pray ...
Omnes sancti Angeli et Archangeli, orate pro nobis	All you holy Angels and Archangels, pray for us
Omnes sancti beatorum Spirituum ordines, orate pro nobis	All you holy orders of blessed Spirits, pray for us
Sancte Joannes Baptista, ora ...	St John the Baptist, pray ...
Sancte Joseph, ora ...	St Joseph, pray ...
Omnes sancti Patriarchæ et Prophetæ, orate pro nobis	All you holy Patriarchs and Prophets, pray for us
Sancte Petre, ora ...	St Peter, pray ...
Sante Paule, ora ...	St Paul, pray ...
Sancte Andrea, ora ...	St Andrew, pray ...
Sancte Jacobe, ora ...	St James the Great, pray ...
Sancte Joannes, ora ...	St John, pray ...
Sancte Thoma, ora ...	St Thomas, pray ...
Sancte Jacobe, ora ...	St James the Less, pray ...
Sancte Philippe, ora ...	St Philip, pray ...
Sancte Bartholomæe, ora ...	St Bartholomew, pray ...
Sancte Matthæe, ora ...	St Matthew, pray ...
Sancte Simon, ora ...	St Simon, pray ...
Sancte Thaddæe, ora ...	St Thaddeus (Jude), pray ...
Sancte Matthia, ora ...	St Matthias, pray ...
Sancte Barnaba, ora ...	St Barnabas, pray ...
Sancte Luca, ora ...	St Luke, pray ...
Sancte Marce, ora ...	St Mark, pray ...
Omnes sancti Apostoli et Evangelistæ, orate pro nobis	All you holy Apostles and Evangelists, pray for us
Omnes sancti Discipuli Domini, orate pro nobis	All you holy Disciples of the Lord, pray for us
Omnes Sancti Innocentes, orate pro nobis	All you holy Innocents, pray for us
Sancte Stephane, ora ...	St Stephen, pray ...
Sancte Laurenti, ora ...	St Lawrence, pray ...
Sancte Vincenti, ora ...	St Vincent of Saragossa, pray ...
Sancti Fabiane et Sebastiane, orate pro nobis	St Fabian and St Sebastian, pray for us

Sancti Joannes et Paule,
orate pro nobis

Sancti Cosma et Damiane,
orate pro nobis

Sancti Gervasi et Protasi,
orate pro nobis

Omnes sancti Martyres,
orate pro nobis

Sancte Silvester, ora ...

Sancte Gregori, ora ...

Sancte Ambrosi, ora ...

Sancte Augustine, ora ...

Sancte Hieronyme, ora ...

Sancte Martine, ora ...

Sancte Nicolae, ora ...

Omnes sancti Pontifices et
Confessores, orate pro nobis

Omnes sancti Doctores,
orate pro nobis

Sancte Antoni, ora ...

Sancte Benedicte, ora ...

Sancte Bernarde, ora ...

Sancte Dominice, ora ...

Sancte Francisce, ora ...

Omnes sancti Sacerdotes et
Levitæ, orate pro nobis

Omnes sancti Monachi et
Eremitæ, orate pro nobis

Sancta Maria Magdalena, ora ...

Sancta Agatha, ora ...

Sancta Lucia, ora ...

Sancta Agnes, ora ...

Sancta Cæcilia, ora ...

Sancta Catharina,
ora ...

Sancta Anastasia, ora ...

Omnes sanctæ Virgines et Viduæ,
orate pro nobis

Omnes Sancti et Sanctæ Dei,
intercedite pro nobis

Propitius esto,
parce nobis, Domine

Propitius esto,
exaudi nos, Domine

Ab omni malo,
libera nos, Domine

St John and St Paul,
pray for us

St Cosmas and St Damian,
pray for us

St Gervase and St Protase
pray for us

All you holy Martyrs,
pray for us

St Sylvester, pray ...

St Gregory the Great, pray ...

St Ambrose, pray ...

St Augustine of Hippo, pray ...

St Jerome, pray ...

St Martin of Tours, pray ...

St Nicholas of Bari, pray ...

All you holy Bishops and
Confessors, pray for us

All you holy Teachers of the
Church, pray for us

St Antony the Hermit, pray ...

St Benedict, pray ...

St Bernard of Clairvaux, pray ...

St Dominic, pray ...

St Francis of Assisi, pray ...

All you holy Priest and
Ministers, pray for us

All you holy Monks and
Hermits, pray for us

St Mary Magdalen, pray ...

St Agatha, pray ...

St Lucy, pray ...

St Agnes, pray

St Cecily, pray ...

St Catherine of Alexandria,
pray ...

St Anastasia, pray ...

All you holy Virgins and
Widows, pray for us

All you Saints of God,
plead for us

Be merciful,
spare us, O Lord

Be merciful,
graciously hear us, O lord

From every evil,
deliver us, O Lord

Ab omni peccato,
  libera nos, Domine
Ab ira tua, libera ...
A subitanea et improvisa morte,
  libera nos, Domine
Ab insidiis diaboli, libera ...
Ab ira, et odio, et omni mala
  voluntate, libera nos, Domine
A spiritu fornicationis
  libera nos, Domine
A fulgure et tempestate, libera ...
A flagello terræmotus,
  libera nos, Domine
A peste, fame et bello,
  libera nos, Domine
A morte perpetua, libera ...
Per mysterium sanctæ Incarnationis
  tuæ, libera nos, Domine
Per Adventum tuum, libera ...
Per Nativitatem tuam, libera ...
Per Baptismum et sanctum
  Ieiunium tuum, libera ...
Per Crucem et Passionem tuam,
  libera nos, Domine
Per Mortem et Sepulturam tuam,
  libera nos, Domine
Per sanctam Resurrectionem tuam,
  libera nos, Domine
Per admirabilem Ascensionem tuam,
  libera nos, Domine
Per adventum Spiritus Sancti
  Paracliti, libera nos Domine
In die iudicii, libera...
Peccatores,
  te rogamus, audi nos
Ut nobis parcas, te rogamus ...
Ut nobis indulgeas,
  te rogamus, audi nos
Ut ad veram poenitentiam nos
  perducere digneris, te rogamus ...
Ut Ecclesiam tuam sanctam regere
  et conservare digneris, te ...

Ut Domnum Apostolicum et omnes
  ecclesiasticos ordines in sancta
  religione conservare digneris, te ...

From every sin,
  deliver us, O Lord
From your anger, deliver ...
From sudden and unforeseen death,
  deliver us, O Lord
From the snares from Satan, deliver ...
From anger, hatred, and all
  ill-will, deliver us, O Lord
From the spirit of uncleanness
  deliver us, O Lord
From lightning and storm, deliver ...
From the scourge of earthquake,
  deliver us, O Lord
From plague, famine and war,
  deliver us, O Lord
From everlasting death, deliver ...
Through the mystery of your
  holy incarnation, deliver ...
Through your coming, deliver ...
Through your birth, deliver ...
Through your baptism and holy
  fasting, deliver us, O Lord
Through your cross and passion
  deliver us, O Lord
Through your death and burial,
  deliver us, O Lord
Through your holy resurrection,
  deliver us, O Lord
Through your wonderful ascension,
  deliver us, O Lord
Through the coming of the Holy
  Spirit, our Advocate, deliver ...
On the day of Judgement, deliver ...
Sinner that we are,
  we beseech you, hear us
That you will spare us, we beseech ...
That you will be merciful,
  we beseech you, hear us
That you will bring us to true
  repentance, we beseech ...
That you will govern and
  preserve your holy Church,
  we beseech ...

That you will keep the successor of Peter
  and all the clergy true to the
  gospel, we beseech ...

Ut inimicos sanctæ Ecclesiæ
humiliare digneris, te rogamus ...

Ut regibus et principibus
christianis pacem et veram
concordiam donare digneris, te ...

Ut cuncto populo christiano
pacem et unitatem largiri
digneris, te rogamus, audi nos

Ut omnes errantes ad unitatem
Ecclesiæ revocare, et infideles
universos ad Evangelii lumen
perducere digneris,
te rogamus ...

Ut nosmetipsos in tuo sancto
servitio confortare et conservare
digneris, te rogamus ...

Ut mentes nostras ad coelestia
desideria erigas, te rogamus ...

Ut omnibus benefactoribus nostris
sempiterna bona retribuas, te ...

Ut animas nostras, fratrum,
propinquorum et benefactorum
nostrorum ab æterna
damnatione eripias, te togamus,
audi nos

Ut fructus terræ dare et
conservare digneris,
te rogamus ...

Ut omnibus fidelibus defunctis
requiem æternam donare
digneris, te rogamus, audi nos

Ut nos exaudire digneris, te ...

Fili Dei, te rogamus ...

Agnus Dei, qui tollis peccata mundi,
parce nobis, Domine

Agnus Dei, qui tollis peccata
mundi, exaudi nos, Domine

Agnus Dei, qui tollis peccata
mundi, miserere nobis

That you will humble the
enemies of holy Church,
we beseech ...

That you will give peace and
true concord to Christian
kings and princes, we beseech ...

That you will grant peace and
unity to all Christians,
we beseech you, hear us

That you will recall to the unity
of the Church all those who
are straying, and lead all
unbelievers to the light of
the gospel, we ...

That we ourselves may be
strengthened and preserved
in your holy service,
we beseech you ...

That you will raise our minds
to desire the things of heaven, we ...

That you will reward all our
benefactors with eternal
blessings, we ...

That you will deliver our souls,
and the souls of our brothers
and sisters, relatives and
benefactors from eternal
damnation, we ...

That you will grant us the fruits
of the earth, and preserve
them, we ...

That you will grant eternal
rest to all the faithful departed,
we beseech you, hear us

That you will graciously hear us, we ...

Son of God, we beseech you hear us.

Lamb of God, you take away
the sins of the world, spare us,
O Lord

Lamb of God, you take away
the sins of the world, graciously
hear us, O Lord

Lamb of God, you take away
the sins of the world, have
mercy on us.

Christe, audi nos
Christe, exaudi nos
Kyrie, eleison
Christe, eleison
Kyrie, eleison.

Pater noster.
Et ne nos inducas in tentationem

Sed libera nos a malo.

Oremus
Deus, a quo sancta desideria,
recta consilia, et justa sunt
opera, da servis tuis illam, quam
mundus dare non potest, pacem:
ut et corda nostra mandatis tuis
dedita, et hostium sublata
formidine, tempora sint tua
protectione tranquilla.

Per Christum Dominum nostrum

Amen.

Christ, hear us
Christ, graciously hear us
Lord, have mercy
Christ, have mercy
Lord, have mercy.

Our Father (in silence)
And lead us not into
    temptation
But deliver us from evil.

Let us pray
O God, the source of all good
desires, all right judgements,
and all just works, give to you
servants that peace which the
world cannot give; that our
hearts may be set to obey your
commandments, and that freed
from fear of our enemies, we may
pass our time in rest and quietness.
We ask this in the name of Christ
    our Lord.
Amen.

SEVEN CHURCHES

The most important churches in Rome, those presided over personally by the pope, have always been the goal of pilgrims: the Lateran, St Peter's, St Paul's, Mary Major and St Lawrence. To these, to make a round seven, were eventually added the church of the Holy Cross, and the catacomb church of St Sebastian, long venerated as the first burial place of Sts Peter and Paul.

The custom of visiting all seven, and of saying prescribed prayers there, grew over the years into an indulgenced devotion, much practised in Holy Week. A walk of 25km was entailed, of which the most taxing part was the long slog outside the walls to St Paul's, across country (the Via delle Sette Chiese) to St Sebastian's, and so back into town. With increasing motorised traffic, the custom has in our own days inevitably declined, but there is no reason why lone enthusiasts should not continue the practice.

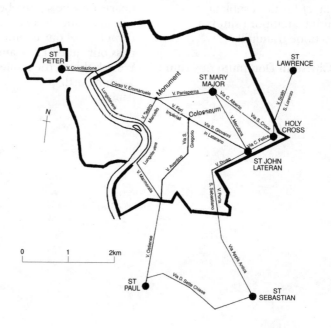

A SELECTION OF HYMNS

(in alphabetical order)

1   Alleluia, sing to Jesus,
his the sceptre, his the throne;
alleluia, his the triumph,
his the victory alone;
hark the songs of peaceful Sion
thunder like a mighty flood:
Jesus, out of every nation,
hath redeemed us by his blood.

Alleluia, not as orphans
are we left in sorrow now;
alleluia, he is near us,
faith believes, nor questions how;
though the cloud from sight received him
when the forty days were o'er,
shall our hearts forget his promise,
'I am with you evermore?'

W. Chatterton Dix

2   All people that on earth do dwell,
sing to the Lord with cheerful voice;
him serve with fear, his praise forth tell,
come ye before him and rejoice.

The Lord, ye know, is God indeed,
without our aid he did us make;
we are his folk, he doth us feed
and for his sheep he doth us take.

O enter then his gates with praise,
approach with joy his courts unto;
praise, laud and bless his name always,
for it is seemly so to do.

To Father, Son and Holy Ghost,
the God whom heaven and earth adore,
from men and from the angel-host
be praise and glory evermore.

Psalm 100, trsl. William Kethe, Day's Psalter

3 Amazing grace! How sweet the sound
that saved a wretch like me.
I once was lost, but now I'm found,
was blind, but now I see.

'Twas grace that taught my heart to fear,
and grace my fears relieved.
How precious did that grace appear
the hour I first believed.

Through many dangers, toils and snares
I have already come.
'Tis grace hath brought me safe thus far,
and grace will lead me home.

The Lord has promised good to me;
his word my hope secures.
He will my shield and portion be
as long as life endures.

John Newton

4 At the name of Jesus
every knee shall bow,
every tongue confess him
King of glory now.
'Tis the Father's pleasure
we should call him Lord,
who from the beginning
was the mighty Word.

Humbled for a season,
to receive a name
from the lips of sinners
unto whom he came,
faithfully he bore it
spotless to the last,
brought it back victorious,
when from death he passed.

Name him, brothers, name him
with love strong as death,
but with awe and wonder,
and with bated breath;
he is God the Saviour,
he is Christ the Lord,

ever to be worshipped,
trusted and adored.

Brothers, this Lord Jesus
shall return again,
with his Father's glory,
with his angel train;
for all wreaths of empire
meet upon his brow,
and our hearts confess him
King of glory now.

Caroline Maria Noel

5   Be still and know that I am God. *(3 times)*

I am the Lord that healeth thee. *(3 times)*

In thee, O Lord, I put my trust. *(3 times)*

6   **Bind us together, Lord, bind us together**
with cords that cannot be broken;
bind us together, Lord, bind us together, Lord,
bind us together with love.

There is only one God
there is only one King,
there is only one Body,
that is why we sing.

Made for the glory of God,
purchased by His precious Son,
born with the right to be clean,
for Jesus the victory has won.

You are the family of God
you are the promise divine,
you are God's chosen desire,
you are the glorious new wine

B. Gillman

7   Blessed assurance – Jesus is mine!
O what a foretaste of glory divine!
Heir of salvation, purchase of God;
born of his Spirit, washed in his blood.

**This is my story, this is my song,
praising my Saviour all the day long.** (Repeat)

Perfect submission, perfect delight,
vision of rapture burst on my sight;
angels descending bring from above
echoes of mercy, whispers of love.

Perfect submission, all is at rest,
I in my Saviour am happy and blest;
watching and waiting, looking above,
filled with his goodness, lost in his love.

Fanny J. Crosby

8   Breathe on me, Breath of God,
fill me with life anew,
that I may love what thou dost love,
and do what thou wouldst do.

Breathe on me, Breath of God,
until my heart is pure:
until with thee I have one will
to do and to endure.

Breathe on me, Breath of God,
till I am wholly thine,
until this earthly part of me
glows with thy fire divine.

Breathe on me, Breath of God,
so shall I never die,
but live with thee the perfect life
of thine Eternity.

Edwin Hatch

9   Christ has died, alleluia,
Christ is risen, alleluia,
Christ will come again, alleluia, alleluia.

10

Crown him with many crowns,
the Lamb upon his throne:
hark how the heavenly anthem drowns
all music but its own.
Awake, my soul, and sing
of him who died for thee,
and hail him as thy matchless King
through all eternity.

Crown him the Lord of life,
who triumphed o'er the grave,
and rose victorious in the strife
for those he came to save.
His glories now we sing
who died and rose on high,
who died eternal life to bring,
and lives that death may die.

Crown him the Lord of love;
behold his hands and side,
rich wounds yet visible above,
in beauty glorified.
All hail, Redeemer, hail!
for thou hast died for me:
thy praise shall never, never fail
throughout eternity.

Matthew Bridges & Godfrey Thring

11

Do not be afraid, for I have redeemed you;
I have called you by your name: you are mine.

When you walk through the waters I'll be with you,
you will never sink beneath the waves.

When the fire is burning all around you,
you will never be consumed by the flames.

When the fear of loneliness is looming,
then remember I am at your side.

When you dwell in the exile of the stranger,
remember you are precious in my eyes.

You are mine, O my child, I am your Father,
and I love you with a perfect love.

Isaiah 43: 1-7, trsl. Gerard Markland

12

For all the saints who from their labours rest,
who thee by faith before the world confest,
thy name, O Jesu be for ever blest.
Alleluia, alleluia!

Thou wast their rock, their fortress, and their might;
thou, Lord, their captain in the well-fought fight;
thou in the darkness drear their one true light.

O may thy soldiers, faithful, true, and bold,
fight as the saints who nobly fought of old,
and win, with them, the victor's crown of gold.

From earth's wide bounds, from ocean's farthest coast,
through gates of pearl streams in the countless host,
singing to Father, Son and Holy Ghost.
William Walsham How

13

Give me joy in my heart, keeping me praising,
give me joy in my heart, I pray.
Give me joy in my heart, keep me praising.
keep me praising till the end of day.

Sing hosanna! Sing hosanna!
Sing hosanna to the King of Kings!
Sing hosanna! Sing hosanna!
Sing hosanna to the King!

Give me peace in my heart, keep me resting ...

Give me love in my heart, keep me serving ...
Traditional

14

Glory to God, glory to God,
glory to the Father.
Glory to God, glory to God,
glory to the Father.
To him be glory for ever.
To him be glory for ever.
Alleluia, amen.
Alleluia, amen,
alleluia, amen,
alleluia, amen.

Glory to God, glory to God,
Son of the Father.

Glory to God, glory to God,
glory to the Spirit.

Peruvian

15 God forgave my sin in Jesus' name;
I've been born again in Jesus' name;
and in Jesus' name I come to you
to share his love as he told me to.

He said: **'Freely, freely, you have received;**
freely, freely give.
Go, in my name, and because you believe,
others will know that I live'.

All pow'r is giv'n in Jesus' name,
in earth and heav'n in Jesus' name;
and in Jesus' name I come to you
to share his pow'r as he told me to.

God gives us life in Jesus' name,
he lives in us in Jesus' name;
and in Jesus' name I come to you
to share his peace as he told me to.

Carol Owens

16 God's Spirit is in my heart:
he has called me and set me apart;
this is what I have to do,
what I have to do.

He's sent me to give the Good News to the poor,
tell prisoners that they are prisoners no more,
tell blind people that they can see,
and set the downtrodden free,
and go tell ev'ryone
the news that the Kingdom of God has come,
and go tell ev'ryone
the news that God's Kingdom has come.

Just as the Father sent me,
so I'm sending you out to be

my witnesses throughout the world.
the whole of the world.

By dying I'm going away,
but I'll be with you every day
as the Spirit of love in your heart,
the love in your heart.

H.J. Richards

17

Guide me, O thou great Redeemer,
pilgrim through this barren land;
I am weak, but thou art mighty,
hold me with thy powerful hand;
Bread of heaven,
feed me till I want no more.

Open now the crystal fountain
whence the healing stream doth flow;
let the fire and cloudy pillar
lead me all my journey through;
strong Deliverer,
be thou still my strength and shield.

When I tread the verge of Jordan,
bid my anxious fears subside;
Death of death, and hell's Destruction,
land me safe on Canaan's side;
songs of praises
I will ever give to thee.

William Williams, trsl. Peter Williams & others

18

Hail, Queen of heav'n, the ocean star,
guide of the wand'rer here below;
thrown on life's surge, we claim thy care;
save us from peril and from woe.
Mother of Christ, star of the sea,
pray for the wanderer, pray for me.

O gentle, chaste and spotless maid,
we sinners make our prayers through thee;
remind thy son that he has paid
the price of our iniquity.
Virgin most pure, star of the sea,
pray for the sinner, pray for me.

Sojourners in this vale of tears,
to thee, blest advocate, we cry;
pity our sorrows, calm our fears,
and soothe with hope our misery.
Refuge in grief, star of the sea,
pray for the mourner, pray for me.

And while to him who reigns above,
in Godhead one, in Persons three,
the source of life, of grace, of love,
homage we pay on bended knee,
do thou, bright Queen, star of the sea,
pray for thy children, pray for me.
John Lingard

19 He did no wrong, he told no lie,
he was silent under the rod;
they cursed him and he kept his peace,
he put his trust in his God.

His were the wounds that healed us. *(3 times)*
Behold the Lamb of God.

His body bore the weight of sin
as he hung and died on the cross,
that we, like him, should die to sin,
and live, as he did, for God.

He suffered so that we should walk
on the very road that he trod;
all we like sheep had gone astray,
till he led us back to God.
1 Peter 2: 22-25, trsl. H.J. Richards

20 He is Lord, he is Lord,
he is risen from the dead and he is Lord.
Every knee shall bow, every tongue confess
that Jesus Christ is Lord.
Traditional

21 He's got the whole world in his hands,
he's got the whole world in his hands,
he's got the whole wide world in his hands,
he's got the whole world in his hands.

He's got you and me, brother, in his hands.

He's got you and me, sister, in his hands.

He's got the little bitty baby in his hands.

Traditional

22　He who would valiant be
'gainst all disaster,
let him in constancy
follow the Master.
There's no discouragement
shall make him once relent
his first avowed intent
to be a pilgrim.

Whoso beset him round
with dismal stories,
do but themselves confound:
his strength the more is.
No foes shall stay his might
though he with giants fight:
he will make good his right
to be a pilgrim.

Since, Lord, thou dost defend
us with thy Spirit,
we know we at the end
shall life inherit.
Then fancies flee away!
I'll fear not what men say,
I'll labour night and day
to be a pilgrim.

Percy Dearmer

23　Holy God we praise thy name;
Lord of all, we bow before thee!
All on earth thy sceptre own,
all in heaven above adore thee.
Infinite thy vast domain,
everlasting is thy reign.

Hark! the loud celestial hymn,
angel choirs above are raising;

Cherubim and Seraphim,
in unceasing chorus praising,
fill the heavens with sweet accord,
holy, holy, holy Lord.

Holy Father, holy Son,
holy Spirit, three we name thee,
while in essence only one
undivided God we claim thee;
and adoring bend the knee,
while we own the mystery.

C.A. Walworth

24　Holy, holy, holy is the Lord,
holy is the Lord God almighty *(twice)*
who was, and is, and is to come;
holy, holy, holy is the Lord.

Blessed, blessed, blessed is the Lord,
blessed is the Lord God almighty *(twice)*
who was, and is, and is to come;
blessed, blessed, blessed is the Lord.

Glory, glory, glory to the Lord,
glory to the Lord God almighty *(twice)*
who was, and is, and is to come;
glory, glory, glory to the Lord.

Anon.

25　Holy, holy, holy! Lord God almighty!
Early in the morning our song shall rise to thee;
holy, holy, holy! Merciful and mighty!
God in three persons, blessed Trinity!

Holy, holy, holy! All the saints adore thee,
casting down their golden crowns around the glassy sea;
Cherubim and Seraphim falling down before thee,
which wert, and art, and evermore shalt be.

Holy, holy, holy! Lord God almighty!
All thy works shall praise thy name, in earth, in sky
　　and sea;
holy, holy, holy! Merciful and mighty!
God in three persons, blessed Trinity!

Reginald Heber

185

26
Holy Spirit, Lord of light,
from the clear celestial height,
thy pure beaming radiance give;
come, thou Father of the poor,
come with treasures which endure;
come, thou light of all that live!

Thou, of all consolers best,
thou, the soul's delightsome guest,
dost refreshing peace bestow:
thou in toil art comfort sweet;
pleasant coolness in the heat;
solace in the midst of woe.

Heal our wounds, our strength renew;
on our dryness pour thy dew;
wash the stains of guilt away:
bend the stubborn heart and will;
melt the frozen, warm the chill;
guide the steps that go astray.

Thou, on those who evermore
thee confess and thee adore,
in thy sevenfold gifts descend:
give them comfort when they die;
give them life with thee on high;
give them joys that never end.

Stephen Langton, trsl. Edward Caswall

27
Holy Virgin, by God's decree,
you were called eternally,
that he could give his Son to our race.
Mary, we praise you, hail, full of grace.
Ave, ave, ave Maria.

By your faith and loving accord,
as the handmaid of the Lord,
you undertook God's plan to embrace.
Mary, we thank you, hail, full of grace.

Joy to God you gave and expressed,
of all women none more blessed,
when in mankind your son took his place.
Mary, we love you, hail, full of grace.

To our needy world of today
love and beauty you portray,
showing the path to Christ we must trace.
Mary, our mother, hail, full of grace.

J-P Lécot, trsl. W.R. Lawrence

28   How lovely on the mountains are the feet of him
who brings good news, good news,
announcing peace, proclaiming news of happiness:
our God reigns, our God reigns!

**Our God reigns, Our God reigns,
our God reigns, our God reigns!**

You watchmen, lift your voices joyfully as one,
shout for your king, your king!
See eye to eye, the Lord restoring Sion:
our God reigns, our God reigns!

Waste–places of Jerusalem, break forth with joy!
We are redeemed, redeemed,
the Lord has saved and comforted his people.
our God reigns, our God reigns!

Isaiah 52: 7-10 , trsl L.E. Smith

29   **I am the resurrection and the life;
those who believe in me will never die.**

I have come to bring the truth;
I have come to bring you life;
if you believe, then you shall live.

In my word the world will come to know,
it is love that makes the spirit grow;
if you believe, then you shall live.

Keep in mind the things that I have said;
remember me in the breaking of the bread;
if you believe, then you shall live.

As my Father created with his breath,
so I too will call you from your death;
if you believe, then you shall live.

Ray Repp & H.J. Richards

30

I danced in the morning when the world was begun,
and I danced in the moon and the stars and the sun,
and I came down from heaven and I danced on the earth,
at Bethlehem I had my birth.

**Dance, then, wherever you may be,
I am the Lord of the Dance, said he.
And I'll lead you all, wherever you may be,
and I'll lead you all in the dance, said he.**

I danced for the scribe and the pharisee,
but they wouldn't dance, and they wouldn't follow me.
I danced for the fishermen, for James and John;
they came with me and the dance went on.

I danced on the Sabbath and I cured the lame:
the holy people, they said it was a shame;
they whipped and they stripped and they hung me on
     high,
and they left me there on the cross to die.

I danced on a Friday when the sun turned black:
it's hard to dance with the Devil on your back;
they buried my body, and they thought I'd gone,
but I am the dance, and I still go on.

They cut me down and I leapt up high:
I am the life that'll never, never die.
I'll live in you if you live in me;
I am the Lord of the Dance, said he.

Sydney Carter

© *1963, 1979 Stainer & Bell Ltd, London, England.*

31

**If God is for us, who can be against,
if the Spirit of God has set us free?**

I know that nothing in this world
can ever take us from his love.

Nothing can take us from his love
poured out in Jesus, the Lord.

And nothing present or to come
can ever take us from his love.

I know that neither death nor life
can ever take us from his love.

Romans 8: 31-39, trsl. John Foley SJ

32

Immortal, invisible, God only wise,
in light inaccessible hid from our eyes,
most blessed, most glorious, the Ancient of Days,
almighty, victorious, thy great name we praise.

Unresting, unhasting, and silent as light,
nor wanting nor wasting, thou rulest in might;
thy justice like mountains high-soaring above
thy clouds which are fountains of goodness and love.

To all life thou givest, to both great and small;
in all life thou livest, the true life of all;
we blossom and flourish as leaves on the tree,
and wither and perish: but naught changeth thee.

Great Father of glory, pure Father of light,
thine angels adore thee, all veiling their sight;
all laud we would render: O help us to see
'tis only the splendour of light hideth thee.

W. Chalmers Smith

33

I will sing, I will sing a song unto the Lord,
I will sing, I will sing a song unto the Lord,
I will sing, I will sing a song unto the Lord,
alleluia, glory to the Lord.

Allelu, alleluia, glory to the Lord (*3 times*)
alleluia, glory to the Lord.

We will come, we will come as one before the Lord (*3 times*)
alleluia, glory to the Lord.

If the Son, if the Son, if the Son shall make you free (*3 times*)
you shall be free indeed.

Ev'ry knee shall bow and ev'ry tongue confess (*3 times*)
that Jesus Christ is Lord.

In his name, in his name we have the victory (*3 times*)
alleluia, glory to the Lord.

Max Dyer

189

34   Jesus Christ is risen today, **Alleluia!**
our triumphant holy day, **Alleluia!**
who did once, upon the cross, **Alleluia!**
suffer to redeem our loss. **Alleluia!**

Hymns of praise then let us sing,
unto Christ our heavenly king,
who endured the cross and grave,
sinners to redeem and save.

But the pains that he endured
our salvation have procured;
now above the sky he's king,
where the angels ever sing.

Lyra Davidica

35   Jesus is Lord, Jesus is Lord, Jesus is Lord, Jesus is Lord.
Alleluia, alleluia, alleluia, alleluia.

And I love him *(4 times)*

Christ is risen *(4 times)*

Send your Spirit *(4 times)*

Alleluia *(4 times)*

Traditional

Copyright © 1982 Springtide. Administered by Copycare, PO Box 77, Hailsham BN27 3EF UK.
Used by permission.

36   Jesus, remember me, when you come into your kingdom;
Jesus, remember me, when you come into your kingdom.
Luke 23: 42

37   Jesus, stand among us in thy risen power;
let this time of worship be a hallowed hour.

Breathe the Holy Spirit into every heart;
bid the fears and sorrows from each soul depart.

Thus with quickened footsteps we'll pursue our way,
watching for the dawning of eternal day.
William Pennefather

38 Keep in mind that Jesus Christ has died for us
and is risen from the dead.
He is our saving Lord.
He is joy for all ages.

Lucien Deiss

39 Kum ba yah, my Lord, kum ba yah!
Kum ba yah, my Lord, kum ba yah!
Kum ba yah, my Lord, kum ba yah!
O Lord, kum ba yah!

Someone's crying, Lord, kum ba yah!

Someone's singing, Lord, kum ba yah!

Someone's praying, Lord, kum ba yah!

Someone's hungry, Lord, kum ba yah!

Someone's suffering, Lord, kum ba yah!

Someone's lonely, Lord, kum ba yah!

Spiritual

40 Lamb of God, you take away the sins of the world;
when we ask your mercy, hear us, O Lord.

Lamb of God, you take away the sins of the world;
when we ask your mercy, hear us, O Lord.

Lamb of God, you take away the sins of the world;
when we ask for your peace, hear us, O Lord.

Damian Lundy

41 Lead, kindly light, amid th'encircling gloom,
lead thou me on;
the night is dark and I am far from home,
lead thou me on.
Keep thou my feet; I do not ask to see
the distant scene; one step enough for me.

I was not ever thus, nor prayed that thou
shouldst lead me on;

I loved to choose and see my path; but now
    lead thou me on.
I loved the garish day, and, spite of fears,
    pride ruled my will; remember not past years.

So long thy power hath blest me, sure it still
    will lead me on
o'er moor and fen, o'er crag and torrent, till
    the night is gone;
and with the morn those angel faces smile
    which I have loved long since, and lost awhile.
                John Henry Newman

42   Let all mortal flesh keep silence
and with fear and trembling stand,
ponder nothing earthly-minded:
for with blessing in his hand,
Christ our God on earth descendeth,
our full homage to demand.

King of kings, yet born of Mary,
as of old on earth he stood,
Lord of lords, in human vesture,
in the Body and the Blood.
He will give to all the faithful
his own self for heavenly food.

Rank on rank the host of heaven
spread its vanguard on the way,
as the Light of Light descendeth
from the realms of endless day,
that the powers of hell may vanish
as the darkness clears away.

At his feet the six-winged Seraphs,
Cherubim with sleepless eye,
veil their faces to the Presence,
as with ceaseless voice they cry,
Alleluia, alleluia,
alleluia, Lord most high.
            Liturgy of St James, trsl. G Moultrie

43   Let all that is within me cry holy.
Let all that is within me cry holy.
Holy, holy, holy is the Lamb that was slain.

Let all that is within me cry mighty.

Let all that is within me cry worthy.

Let all that is within me cry blessed.

Let all that is within me cry Jesus.

Let all that is within me cry risen.

Traditional

44
Let all the world in every corner sing,
'My God and King!'
The heavens are not too high,
his praise may thither fly:
the earth is not too low,
his praises there may grow.
Let all the world in every corner sing,
'My God and King!'

Let all the world in every corner sing,
'My God and King!'
The Church with psalms must shout,
no door can keep them out:
but, above all, the heart
must bear the longest part.
Let all the world in every corner sing,
'My God and King!'

George Herbert

45
Let there be peace shared among us,
let there be peace in our eyes;
may now your peace sweep this nation –
cause us, O Lord, to arise.
Give us a fresh understanding,
brotherly love that is real.
Let there be peace shared among us,
let there be peace.

Dave Bilbrough

46
Let us break bread together on our knees.
Let us break bread together on our knees.
When I fall on my knees with my face to the rising sun,
O Lord, have mercy on me.

Let us drink wine together on our knees.

Let us praise God together on our knees.
Traditional

47   Living, he loved me; dying, he saved me;
buried, he carried my sins far away;
rising, he justified freely for ever;
one day he's coming – O glorious day!
Traditional

48   Low in the grave he lay, Jesus, my Saviour,
waiting the coming day, Jesus, my Lord.

**Up from the grave he arose,
with a mighty triumph o'er his foes:
he arose a victor from the dark domain,
and he lives for ever with his saints to reign:
he arose! he arose! hallelujah! Christ arose!**

Vainly they watch his bed, Jesus, my Saviour,
vainly they seal the dead, Jesus, my Lord.

Death cannot keep his prey, Jesus, my Saviour:
he tore the bars away, Jesus, my Lord.
Robert Lowry

49   Make me a channel of your peace:
where there is hatred, let me bring your love;
where there is injury, your pardon, Lord,
and where there's doubt, true faith in you.

Make me a channel of your peace:
where there's despair in life, let me bring hope;
where there is darkness, only light,
and where there's sadness, ever joy.

O Master, grant that I may never seek
so much to be consoled as to console,
to be understood as to understand,
to be loved as to love with all my soul.

Make me a channel of your peace:
it is in pardoning that we are pardoned,

in giving to all men that we receive,
and in dying that we're born to eternal life.
Sebastian Temple

50 Now the green blade riseth from the buried grain,
wheat that in the dark earth many days has lain;
love lives again, that with the dead has been:
love is come again like wheat that springeth green.

In the grave they laid him, love whom men had slain,
thinking that never he would wake again,
laid in the earth like grain that sleeps unseen:
love is come again like wheat that springeth green.

Forth he came at Easter, like the risen grain,
he that for three days in the grave had lain,
quick from the dead my risen Lord is seen:
love is come again like wheat that springeth green.

When our hearts are wintry, grieving or in pain,
thy touch can call us back to life again,
fields of our heart that dead and bare have been:
love is come again like wheat that springeth green.
J.M.C. Crum

51 O come, all ye faithful, joyful and triumphant,
O come ye, O come ye to Bethlehem;
come and behold him, born the king of angels:

O come, let us adore him,
O come, let us adore him,
O come, let us adore him,
Christ the Lord.

True God of true God, Light of Light eternal,
lo! He abhors not the Virgin's womb;
Very God, begotten, not created:

Sing, choirs of angels, sing in exultation,
sing, all ye citizens of heaven above,
Glory to God in the highest:

Yea, Lord, we greet thee, born this happy morning:
Jesus, to thee be glory given,
Word of the Father, now in flesh appearing:
Anon., trsl. Frederick Oakley

52   O for a thousand tongues, to sing
my dear Redeemer's praise,
the glories of my God and King,
the triumphs of his grace!

Jesus! the name that charms our fears,
that bids our sorrows cease;
'tis music in the sinner's ears,
'tis life, and health, and peace.

See all your sins on Jesus laid;
the Lamb of God was slain,
his soul was once an offering made
for every soul of man.

My gracious Master and my God,
assist me to proclaim,
to spread through all the earth abroad
the honours of thy name.

Charles Wesley

53   O God, our help in ages past,
our hope for years to come,
our shelter from the stormy blast,
and our eternal home.

Beneath the shadow of thy throne,
thy saints have dwelt secure;
sufficient is thine arm alone,
and our defence is sure.

Before the hills in order stood,
or earth received her frame,
from everlasting thou art God,
to endless years the same.

O God, our help in ages past,
our hope for years to come,
be thou our guard while troubles last,
and our eternal home.

Isaac Watts

54   **O living water, refresh my soul,
O living water, refresh my soul;
Spirit of joy, Lord of creation,
Spirit of hope, Spirit of peace.**

Spirit of God, Spirit of God.

O set us free, O set us free.

Come pray in us, come pray in us.
Sister Virginia Vissing, SSMN

55
O Lord, my God, when I in awesome wonder,
consider all the worlds thy hand has made,
I see the stars, I hear the rolling thunder,
thy pow'r throughout the universe displayed.

Then sings my soul, my Saviour God, to thee:
How great thou art, how great thou art *(Repeat)*

And when I think that God, his Son not sparing,
sent him to die, I scarce can take it in,
that on the cross, my burden gladly bearing,
he bled and died to take away my sin.

When Christ shall come with shout of acclamation
and take me home, what joy shall fill my heart;
when I shall bow in humble adoration,
and there proclaim: My God, how great thou art!
Stuart K. Hine

56
Once in royal David's city
stood a lowly cattle shed,
where a mother laid her baby
in a manger for his bed:
Mary was that Mother mild,
Jesus Christ her little child.

He came down to earth from heaven
who is God and Lord of all,
and his shelter was a stable
and his cradle was a stall;
with the poor, and mean, and lowly,
lived on earth our Saviour holy.

Not in that poor lowly stable,
with the oxen standing by,
we shall see him; but in heaven,
set at God's right hand on high;

when like stars his children crowned
all in white shall wait around.

Cecil Frances Alexander

57 O worship the Lord in the beauty of holiness,
bow down before him, his glory proclaim;
with gold of obedience, and incense of lowliness,
kneel and adore him, the Lord is his name.

Low at his feet lay thy burden of carefulness,
high on his heart he will bear it for thee,
comfort thy sorrow and answer thy prayerfulness,
guiding thy steps as may best for thee be.

Fear not to enter his courts in the slenderness
of the poor wealth thou would'st reckon as thine;
truth in its beauty, and love in its tenderness,
these are the offerings to lay on his shrine.

These, though we bring them in trembling and
    fearfulness,
he will accept for the name that is dear:
mornings of joy give for evenings of tearfulness,
trust for our trembling, and hope for our fear.

John Samuel Bewley Monsell

58 Peace is flowing like a river,
flowing out through you and me,
spreading out into the desert,
setting all the captives free.

Love is flowing like a river.

Joy is flowing like a river.

Hope is flowing like a river.

Anon.

59 Praise him, praise him,
praise him in the morning,
praise him in the noontime.
Praise him, praise him,
praise him when the sun goes down.

Love him, love him.

Trust him, trust him.

Serve him, serve him.

Jesus, Jesus.

Anon.

60   Praise, my soul, the King of heaven,
to his feet thy tribute bring;
ransomed, healed, restored, forgiven,
who like me his praise should sing?
Praise him! Praise him!
Praise him! Praise him!
Praise the everlasting King.

Praise him for his grace and favour
to our fathers in distress;
praise him, still the same for ever,
slow to chide and swift to bless.
Praise him! Praise him!
Praise him! Praise him!
Glorious in his faithfulness.

Father-like, he tends and spares us:
well our feeble frame he knows;
in his hands he gently bears us,
rescues us from all our foes.
Praise him! Praise him!
Praise him! Praise him!
Widely as his mercy flows.

Angels, help us to adore him:
ye behold him face to face;
sun and moon, bow down before him.
dwellers all in time and space.
Praise him! Praise him!
Praise him! Praise him!
Praise with us the God of grace.

Henry Francis Lyte

61   Praise to the Holiest in the height,
and in the depth be praise;

in all his words most wonderful,
most sure in all his ways!

O loving wisdom of our God!
When all was sin and shame,
a second Adam to the fight
and to the rescue came.

O wisest love! That flesh and blood,
which did in Adam fail,
should strive afresh against the foe,
should strive and should prevail

O generous love! That he who smote
in man for man the foe,
the double agony in man
for man should undergo.

Praise to the Holiest in the height,
and in the depth be praise;
in all his words most wonderful,
most sure in all his ways!

John Henry Newman

62   Praise we our God with joy
and gladness never ending,
angels and saints with us
their grateful voices blending.
He is our Father dear,
o'erfilled with parent's love;
mercies unsought, unknown,
he showers from above.

He is our shepherd true
with watchful care unsleeping,
on us, his erring sheep,
an eye of pity keeping;
he, with a mighty arm,
the bonds of sin doth break,
and to our burdened hearts
in words of peace doth speak.

Graces in copious stream
from that pure fount are welling,
where, in our heart of hearts,

our God hath set his dwelling.
His word our lantern is,
his peace our comfort still,
his sweetness all our rest,
our law, our life, his will.

Frederick Oakeley

63   Rejoice in the Lord always,
and again I say, Rejoice.
Rejoice in the Lord always,
and again I say, Rejoice.
Rejoice, rejoice, and again I say, Rejoice.
Rejoice, rejoice, and again I say, Rejoice.

Philippians 4: 4

64   Seek ye first the kingdom of God
and his righteousness,
and all these things shall be added unto you,
allelu, alleluia.
Alleluia. *(5 times)*

Ask and it shall be given unto you,
seek and ye shall find,
knock and the door will be opened unto you,
allelu, alleluia.

Therefore consider the lilies of the field:
they neither toil nor spin,
yet even Solomon was not arrayed like them,
allelu, alleluia.

If God then clothes all the flowers of the field,
though they will soon die away,
will he not also provide for you as well?
allelu, alleluia.

Matthew 6: 28-7: 7, trsl. H.J. Richards

65   Silent night, holy night,
all is calm, all is bright,
round yon virgin mother and child:
holy infant so tender and mild:
sleep in heavenly peace,
sleep in heavenly peace.

Silent night, holy night;
shepherds quake at the sight,
glories stream from heaven afar,
heavenly hosts sing alleluia:
Christ the Saviour is born,
Christ the Saviour is born.

Silent night, holy night;
Son of God, love's pure light
radiant beams from thy holy face,
with the dawn of redeeming grace:
Jesus, Lord, at thy birth,
Jesus, Lord at thy birth.

Joseph Mohr, trsl J. Young

66 **Sing my soul, sing my soul, sing my soul of his mercy.**
Sing my soul, sing my soul, sing my soul of his mercy.

The Lord is good to me,
his light will shine on me,
when city lights would blind my eyes;
he hears my silent call,
his hands help when I fall,
his gentle voice stills my sighs.

The Lord is good to me,
his word will set me free,
when men would tie me to the ground;
he mocks my foolish ways,
with love that never fails;
when I'm most lost, then I'm found.

The Lord is good to me,
I hear him speak to me,
his voice is in the rain that falls;
he whispers in the air
of his unending care;
if I will hear, then he calls.

Michael Cockett

67 Sing of Mary, pure and lowly,
virgin mother undefiled;
sing of God's own Son most holy,
who became her little child.

Fairest child of fairest mother,
God, the Lord, who came to earth,
Word made flesh, our very brother,
takes our nature by his birth.

Sing of Jesus, son of Mary,
in the home at Nazareth;
toil and labour cannot weary
love enduring unto death.
Constant was the love he gave her,
though he went forth from her side,
forth to preach and heal and suffer,
till on Calvary he died.

Glory be to God the Father,
glory be to God the Son,
glory be to God the Spirit,
glory to the three in one.
From the heart of blessed Mary,
from all saints the song ascends,
and the Church the strain re-echoes
unto earth's remotest ends.

Roland F. Palmer

68   Soul of my Saviour, sanctify my breast;
Body of Christ, be thou my saving guest;
Blood of my Saviour, bathe me in thy tide,
wash me with water flowing from thy side.

Strength and protection may thy Passion be,
O blessed Jesus, hear and answer me;
deep in thy wounds, Lord, hide and shelter me,
so shall I never, never part from thee.

Guard and defend me from the foe malign;
in death's dread moments make me only thine;
call me and bid me come to thee on high,
when I may praise thee with thy saints for aye.

Pope John XXII, trsl. Anon.

69   Spirit of the living God,
fall afresh on me.
Spirit of the living God,
fall afresh on me.
Break me, melt me,

mould me, fill me.
Spirit of the living God,
fall afresh on me.

Daniel Iverson

70   **Take our bread, we ask you,**
take our hearts, we love you,
take our lives, O Father, we are yours,
we are yours.

Yours as we stand at the table you set,
yours as we eat the bread our hearts can't forget;
we are the signs of your life with us yet:
we are yours, we are yours.

Your holy people stand washed in your blood;
Spirit-filled yet hungry, we await your food;
poor though we are, we have brought ourselves to you:
we are yours, we are yours.

Joseph Wise

71   Tell out, my soul, the greatness of the Lord!
Unnumbered blessings give my spirit voice;
tender to me the promise of his word;
in God my Saviour shall my heart rejoice.

Tell out, my soul, the greatness of his name!
Make known his might, the deeds his arm has done;
his mercy sure, from age to age the same;
his holy name: the Lord, the Mighty One.

Tell out, my soul, the greatness of his might!
Powers and dominions lay their glory by;
proud hearts and stubborn wills are put to flight,
the hungry fed, the humble lifted high.

Tell out, my soul, the glories of his word!
Firm is his promise, and his mercy sure.
Tell out, my soul, the greatness of the Lord
to children's children and for evermore!

Timothy Dudley-Smith

72   The Lord's my shepherd, I'll not want;
he makes me down to lie

in pastures green. He leadeth me
the quiet waters by.

My soul he doth restore again,
and me to walk doth make
within the paths of righteousness,
e'en for his own name's sake.

Yea, though I walk in death's dark vale,
yet will I fear none ill,
for thou art with me, and thy rod
and staff me comfort still.

My table thou hast furnishèd
in presence of my foes,
my head thou dost with oil anoint,
and my cup overflows.

Goodness and mercy all my life
shall surely follow me,
and in God's house for evermore
my dwelling place shall be.
Psalm 23, trsl. Scottish Psalter

73   Thine be the glory, risen, conquering Son,
endless is the victory thou o'er death hast won;
angels in bright raiment rolled the stone away,
kept the folded grave-clothes, where thy body lay.

**Thine be the glory, risen, conquering Son,
endless is the victory thou o'er death hast won.**

Lo! Jesus meets us, risen from the tomb:
lovingly he greets us, scatters fear and gloom;
let the Church with gladness hymns of triumph sing,
for her Lord now liveth, death hath lost its sting.
Edmond Budry, trsl. Richard Birch Hoyle

74   This is the day (This is the day)
that the Lord has made (that the Lord has made).
Let us rejoice (Let us rejoice)
and be glad in it (and be glad in it).
This is the day that the Lord has made.
Let us rejoice and be glad in it.

This is the day (This is the day)
that the Lord has made.

This is the day that he rose again.

This is the day that the Spirit came.

Anon.

75 This joyful Eastertide, away with sin and sorrow;
my love, the Crucified, hath sprung to life this morrow.

**Had Christ, that once was slain,
ne'er burst his three-day prison,
our faith had been in vain:
but now hath Christ arisen.**

My flesh in hope shall rest and for a season slumber,
till trump from east to west shall wake the dead in
number.

Death's flood hath lost its chill since Jesus crossed the
river:
Lover of souls, from ill my passing soul deliver.

George Ratcliff Woodward

76 Thou wilt keep him in perfect peace *(3 times)*
whose mind is stayed on thee.

Marvel not, I say unto you *(3 times)*
you must be born again.

Though your sins as scarlet be *(3 times)*
they shall be white as snow.

If the Son shall set you free *(3 times)*
you shall be free indeed.

Anon.

77 To God be the glory! Great things he hath done!
So loved he the world that he gave us his Son,
who yielded his life an atonement for sin,
and opened the life-gate that all may go in.

**Praise the Lord! Praise the Lord!
Let the earth hear his voice!**

Praise the Lord! Praise the Lord!
Let the people rejoice!
O come to the Father through Jesus the Son,
and give him the glory: great things he hath done!

O perfect redemption, the purchase of blood!
To every believer the promise of God;
and every offender who truly believes,
that moment from Jesus a pardon receives.

Great things he hath taught us, great things he hath
    done,
and great our rejoicing through Jesus the Son;
but purer and higher and greater will be
our wonder, our rapture, when Jesus we see!

Fanny J. Crosby

78 **Walk in the light, walk in the light,**
walk in the light, walk in the light of the Lord.

The Spirit lives to set us free,
walk, walk in the light;
he binds us all in unity,
walk, walk in the light.

Jesus promised life to all ...
the dead were wakened by his call ...

He died in pain on Calvary ...
to save the lost like you and me ...

We know his death was not the end ...
he gave his Spirit to be our friend ...

By Jesus' love our wounds are healed ...
the Father's kindness is revealed ...

The Spirit lives in you and me ...
his light will shine for all to see ...

Damian Lundy

79 Were you there when they crucified my Lord?
Were you there when they crucified my Lord?
O, sometimes it causes me to tremble, tremble, tremble!
Were you there when they crucified my Lord?

Were you there when they nailed him to the tree?

Were you there when they pierced him in the side?

Were you there when they laid him in the tomb?

Were you there when God raised him from the dead?
Spiritual

Sts Peter and Paul

80   What fairer light is this than time itself doth own,
the golden day with beams more radiant brightening?
The princes of God's Church this feastday doth
        enthrone,
to sinners heavenward bound their burden lightening.

One taught mankind its creed, one guards the heavenly
        gate;
founders of Rome, they bind the world in loyalty.
One by the sword achieved, one by the cross his fate;
with laurelled brows they hold eternal royalty.

Rejoice, O Rome, this day; thy walls they once did sign
with princely blood, who now their glory share with thee.
What city's vesture glows with crimson deep as thine?
What beauty else has earth that may compare with thee?

To God the three in One eternal homage be,
all honour, all renown, all songs victorious,
who rules both heaven and earth by one divine decree,
to everlasting years in empire glorious.
Elpis, wife of Boethius, trsl. R.A. Knox

81   When I needed a neighbour, were you there, were you
        there?
When I needed a neighbour, were you there?
And the creed and the colour and the name won't matter,
Were you there?

I was hungry and thirsty, were you there, were you there?

I was cold, I was naked, were you there, were you there?

When I needed a shelter, were you there, were you there?

When I needed a healer, were you there, were you there?

Wherever you travel, I'll be there, I'll be there,
wherever you travel, I'll be there.
And the creed and the colour and the name won't matter,
I'll be there.

Sydney Carter

82 When I survey the wondrous cross
on which the Prince of glory died,
my richest gain I count but loss,
and pour contempt on all my pride.

See from his head, his hands his feet,
sorrow and love flow mingled down;
did e'er such love and sorrow meet,
or thorns compose so rich a crown?

Were the whole realm of nature mine,
that were an offering far too small;
love so amazing, so divine,
demands my soul, my life, my all.

Isaac Watts

83 Word made flesh, Son of God,

Come, Lord Jesus, come again.
Come, Lord Jesus, come again.

Lord and Saviour, Son of God.

Prince of Peace, Son of God.

Alleluia, Son of God.

Bread of Life, Son of God.

Light of the World, Son of God.

Jesus Christ, Son of God.

Sister Virginia Vissing, SSMN

INDEX OF BIBLE TEXTS

INDEX OF PLACES

Rome is the ideal mother.
She has too many children,
and being unable to take care of any of them,
she doesn't ask anything of you or expect anything of you.
She welcomes you when you come,
and lets you go when you leave.
Federico Fellini